MATH DETECTIVE™ Beginning

Higher-Order Thinking·Reading·Writing in Mathematics

SERIES TITLES

Math Detective™ Beginning

Math Detective™ A1

Math Detective™ B1

Terri Husted

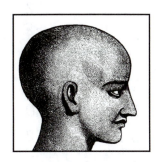

© 2003
CRITICAL THINKING BOOKS & SOFTWARE
www.CriticalThinking.com
P.O. Box 448 • Pacific Grove • CA 93950-0448
Phone 800-458-4849 • FAX 831-393-3277
ISBN 0-89455-802-1
Printed in the United States of America
Reproduction rights granted for single-classroom use only.

TABLE OF CONTENTS

What is Math Detective? iv

Key Ideas and Math Topics Charts vi

Scoring Rubric/Assessment Criteria viii

To the Student: Why You Should Become a Math Detective ix

Sample Problem: The Small Furniture Store x

Math Detective Certificate xiii

I. NUMBER AND NUMERATION

   1—Latoya's Vacation 2
   2—Eddy's Dog Shadow 4
   3—Who's Telling the Truth? 6
   4—School Supplies 8
   5—At the Math Fair 10
   6—The Super Deli 12
   7—The Party Favors 14
   8—The Five Wealthy Women 16
   9—Leafy Lengths 18

II. PATTERNS

   10—The Family Tree 20
   11—Trip to the Theater 22
   12—The Toy Factory 24
   13—The 35¢ Yummy Bar 26

III. OPERATIONS

   14—The City Bus 30
   15—Eddy's Achy Ride 32
   16—An Apple a Day 34
   17—Time to Buy a New Clock 36
   18—The Toy Sale 38
   19—Dinner with Ramón 40
   20—Mr. Papas at the Toy Store 42

IV. GEOMETRY

    21—Off to the State Fair 46

    22—Luis's Letter 48

    23—Annie's Angles Report 50

    24—Trip to the Skating Rink 52

    25—The Pastry Shop 54

    26—Geometry Art 57

V. PROBABILITY

    27—The Color Spinner 60

    28—The Ice Cream Party 62

    29—Summer Reading 64

    30—The Missing Symbols 66

VI. STATISTICS

    31—Mrs. Applecrumb's Famous Fruit Pies 70

    32—Tully Tallies Temper Tantrums 72

    33—The Pet Shelter 74

    34—The Great Fruit Sale 76

    35—Time for Homework 78

    36—Zooey Competition 80

    37—The Basset Hound Bus Company 82

    38—The Shoe Count 84

ANSWERS 87

What is Math Detective?

Introduction

The problems in this book will improve your students' skills in mathematics, critical thinking, reading, and writing. The topics and skills covered are drawn from the national standards for mathematics for grades 3-4 as outlined by the National Council of Teachers of Mathematics. The problems are short, easy to use, and fun for students.

Problem solutions involve critical thinking and careful reading of text, charts, graphs, and tables. Students are required to explain their thinking in writing.

Students are frequently asked to support their answers with evidence. The evidence cannot be uncovered by scanning the text, but instead requires in-depth analysis of the information in the text, diagram, or both. This analysis develops good reading comprehension and critical thinking skills.

The questions in *Math Detective*™ are modeled after questions found on new math assessments, but require more critical thinking. These problems are excellent preparation for assessments that require students to explain and support their answers.

Also included are a chart of key ideas and topics, as well as all answers and solutions.

When to Use The Math Detective™

Math Detective™ can be used to help introduce or review topics in your math curriculum. *Math Detective*™ is an ideal solution for test preparation because it does not teach to a particular assessment. It develops the skills needed to excel on new assessments. In my field-testing with students in grades 3-4, *Math Detective*™ was highly effective in clarifying topics that they had found confusing in previous years. It is also a wonderful source of enrichment activities.

Grades 3-4 Math Standards

The math topics covered in this book are organized around the strands outlined by the National Council of Teachers of Mathematics: Number and Numeration, Patterns, Operations, Geometry and Spatial Sense, Probability, and Statistics. For a detailed list of all topics covered within each of the key ideas, please see the Table of Contents (page ii) or the Key Ideas and Math Topics chart (page vi).

Many problems contain important math vocabulary. Some of these terms are defined in the problem and some must be identified through context clues in the story.

Reading in Mathematics

Many math students have trouble reading in general, and do not understand the importance of reading in mathematics. *Math Detective*™ teaches students to read carefully by requiring the students to identify evidence that supports their answers. In fact, students must often identify information from multiple sources (text, diagrams, and other graphics) and synthesize these different pieces of information to arrive at the answer. The depth of analysis needed to solve these problems develops thinking skills and improves reading comprehension.

Written Explanations

Many questions in this book ask students to use complete sentences to explain their thinking. The ability to express their thoughts—supported by evidence—in writing, is not only important in math assessments, it is essential when communicating with other people in school and work. It also promotes better understanding of the mathematics being studied.

The questions in *Math Detective*™ are modeled after questions found on math assessments but require more critical thinking. Despite the growing trend to evaluate written explanations and support of solutions, many math students score poorly on these test items. The carefully designed questions in *Math Detective*™ will develop thinking, reading, and writing skills while they prepare your students for new state math assessments.

If a student has trouble writing about how she solved a problem, ask her to explain her solution aloud, then guide her on how to write the explanation. Remember, it helps to model your own thinking on how you solved the problem and then ask the student to model her own thinking. Showing work in a neat and organized fashion is also stressed. A separate introduction and sample problem with solutions has been provided for the student.

Thinking Cap Questions

Some problems are questions that go beyond the literal and, at times, interpretive levels of thinking. Such problems are designated by a detective cap, as shown.

KEY IDEAS and MATH TOPICS

NUMBER & NUMERATION

Topic	1. Latoya's Vacation	2. Eddy's Dog	3. Who's Telling	4. School Supplies	5. At the Math Fair	6. The Super Deli	7. The Party Favors	8. Wealthy Women	9. Leafy Lengths
Addition/Subtraction			X	X	X	X		X	
Calendar Concepts	X								
Commutative Property			X						
Division			X			X			
Factors				X					
Fraction Concepts		X							
Graphing Decimals							X		
Money Sense					X	X			
Multiples						X			
Multiplication		X		X	X		X		
Odds/Evens					X				
Place Value						X			
Prime Numbers				X					
Reading Numbers						X			
Timeline Concepts	X								

PATTERNS

Topic	10. The Family Tree	11. Trip to the Theatre	12. The Toy Factory	13. The Yummy Bar
Addition	X	X	X	X
Logic	X	X	X	X
Money Sense		X		X
Multiplication	X	X	X	

OPERATIONS

Topic	14. The City Bus	15. Eddy's Achy Ride	16. An Apple a Day	17. Time to Buy	18. The Toy Sale	19. Dinner w. Ramon	20. Mr. Papas
Addition: Whole Numbers	X	X			X	X	X
Subtraction: Whole Numbers	X	X	X		X	X	X
Multiplication: Whole Numbers				X			X
Division: Whole Numbers							X
Associative Property				X			
Addition: Decimals				X	X		
Subtraction: Decimals				X	X		
Fraction (+ or x)		X					X
Money Sense				X	X	X	

Synthesis
Combines information from multiple sources to draw conclusions.

1	2	3	4	5	6	7	8	9	10	11	12	13	14	15	16	17	18	19	20
	X	X	X	X	X					X				X			X	X	X

Other Math Topics

Number & Numeration

Topic	1	2	3	4	5	6	7	8	9
Vocabulary			X	X					
Estimating			X		X				
Reading or Making Chart						X			

Patterns

Topic	10	11	12	13
Vocabulary			X	
Reading or Making Chart	X		X	X

Operations

Topic	14	15	16	17	18	19	20
Vocabulary			X				
Estimating				X			
Multicultural					X		
Measurement		X					
Reading or Making Chart	X	X	X				X
Time Concepts	X						X
Working Backwards		X					

KEY IDEAS and MATH TOPICS, cont.

GEOMETRY

	Off to State Fair (21)	Luis' Letter (22)	Annie's Angles (23)	Trip to Skating (24)	Pastry Shop (25)	Geometry Art (26)
Angles			X	X		
Area		X				
Coordinate Plane	X	X				
Identifying 3D Shapes					X	
Parallel and Perpendicular			X			
Perimeter		X				
Polygons					X	
Reading or Making a Chart				X	X	

PROBABILITY

	Color Spinner (27)	Ice Cream Party (28)	Summer Reading (29)	Missing Symbols (30)
The Counting Principle		X		
Division Concept				X
Equation Concepts				X
Finding Odds	X	X	X	X
Listing Combinations	X	X		

STATISTICS

	Mrs. A's Pies (31)	Tully Tallies (32)	Pet Shelter (33)	Great Fruit Sale (34)	Time Homework (35)	Zooey Compet. (36)	Basset H'nd Bus (37)	The Shoe Count (38)
Bar Graphs	X		X		X			
Keeping Tallies	X							
Line Graphs		X	X	X				
Misleading Graphs						X		
Pictographs	X							
Survey Basics	X							
Reading or Making a Chart			X				X	X

Synthesis Combines information from multiple sources to draw conclusions.

| GEOMETRY | | X | X X | | X | | PROBABILITY | X X | | X | | STATISTICS | X X | | X X X X X |

Geometry synthesis X's: cols 22, 23, 24, 26
Probability synthesis X's: cols 27, 28, 30
Statistics synthesis X's: cols 31, 32, 34, 35, 36, 37, 38

Other Math Topics

Geometry section (21–26)

	21	22	23	24	25	26
Addition: Whole Numbers		X				
Vocabulary	X	X	X	X	X	X
Measurement		X				
Time Concepts			X			
Whole Numbers Operations		X				

Probability section (27–30)

	27	28	29	30
Decimals (+ or x)	X			
Vocabulary		X		
Measurement		X		
Fraction Concepts			X	
Whole Numbers Operations	X	X		X

Statistics section (31–38)

	31	32	33	34	35	36	37	38
Decimals (x or ÷)	X		X					
Logical Reasoning								X
Measurement				X				
Time Concepts						X	X	
Whole Numbers Operations	X							X

SCORING RUBRIC/ASSESSMENT CRITERIA

Each complete *Math Detective*™ activity includes a story and questions related to that story. Questions may require arithmetic computation, identification of evidence, and explanations of the student's thinking. Therefore, to get a good picture of the student's overall performance on an activity, a 3-part scoring rubric is suggested. First, mark individual questions to indicate errors in computation, identification of evidence, and clarity of the explanations. Using a photocopy of the rubric below, combine the informal assessments to generate an overall 3-part score for the activity.

✂--

Student Name _____

Activity: _____

THREE-CATEGORY SCORING RUBRIC
- Concept understanding (student understands concept, recognizes patterns)
- Clarity of student's explanations (complete sentences, clearly written)
- Correct computation of answers (accuracy of arithmetic computation)

Content: If the information in your answer showed complete understanding of the information in the story and graphics, you got a 3. If it showed a partial understanding, you got a 2 or 1. If there was absolutely no evidence that you understood the information, you got a 0.

Clarity: If you communicated clearly, even if the ideas themselves were wrong, you got a 3. If your ideas were communicated poorly, you got a 1 or 2. If you were not clear and it was impossible to understand your thoughts, you got a 0.

Accuracy: If the computation for all arithmetic problems was correct, you got a 3. If only some of it was correct, you got a 1 or 2. If none of it was correct, you got a 0.

Content Score: _____ (Scale 0–3)
Clarity Score: _____ (Scale 0–3)
Accuracy Score: _____ (Scale 0–3)

Comments:

_____

_____

_____

_____

To the Student

Why You Should Become a Math Detective™

Critical thinking, reading, and writing are as important in mathematics as they are in the rest of your subjects. This workbook was created to improve your thinking, reading, and writing skills while you learn and practice math!

It's All About Evidence

As a critical thinker, you need to look for *evidence* in what you read. Evidence is information that shows why something is true or could be true. Read the six sentences below and try to find the evidence that tells you who was into the peanut butter and jam.

^{1}Eddie's mom looked at Eddie and baby sister Sarah. ^{2}There were crumbs on the floor, and Sarah had peanut butter and jam on her chin. ^{3}"Who got into the peanut butter and jam?" asked Eddie's mom. ^{4}Eddie told his mom that it was little Sarah who had eaten the peanut butter and jam. ^{5}He quickly grabbed a paper towel and put some water on it so his mother could wipe Sarah's chin. ^{6}As he handed the towel to his mother, she noticed peanut butter and jam on Eddie's fingers.

Information in sentence 2 tell us that that "Sarah had peanut butter and jam on her chin." We know from this evidence that she was into the peanut butter and jam. Sentence 6 tells us that Eddie had peanut butter and jam on his fingers. We know from this evidence that Eddie was into the peanut butter and jam. The evidence in sentences 2 and 6 shows us that both Eddie and Sarah were into the peanut butter and jam.

The questions in these activities sometimes ask for the sentence(s) that provide the best evidence for an answer. To help you identify a particular sentence, all the sentences in the stories of this workbook are numbered. Some questions may require you to give the numbers of one or two sentences AND find information from a diagram to answer the question. You may have to go back and search the text or story for the sentence or sentences that contain the evidence you need to prove your answer is correct. All critical thinkers reread what they have read to make sure they understood what was said and to be sure they did not miss any information. In this book, YOU ARE THE DETECTIVE; that is why this book is called *Math Detective*™.

Sample Problem

The Small Furniture Store

[1]Mr. Sands owns a small furniture store where he only makes chairs and stools. [2]He cuts all the wood with a saw and carefully sands every piece by hand. [3]Each chair takes 4 leg pieces and each stool takes 3 leg pieces. [4]Mrs. Sands writes down each week how many pieces of wood her husband uses.

[5]One day Mr. Sands tells Mrs. Sands, "I'm so happy. [6]I have an order to make three chairs and four stools." [7]Mrs. Sands says, "You have enough wood cut out for the seats, but you only have 20 leg pieces left." [8]Mr. Sand replied, "Oh no, I thought I had 24 leg pieces!" [9]Mrs. Sands looked at Mr. Sands and said, "Dear, remember the four-legged table you made for me? [10]If you need 4 leg pieces, take them from the table you made me." [11]Mr. Sand smiled and said, "Thank you, honey, order more wood so I can replace the legs on that table I made you and also make you a beautiful rocking chair."

Questions

1. How many leg pieces are needed for one chair and one stool? _____

   Give the numbers of the two sentences that provide the best evidence for your answer. _____, _____

Solution

   7. Sentence 3. (Sentence 3 tells how many leg pieces each chair and stool need.)

   _____

2. How many leg pieces are needed for 3 chairs and 4 stools? Use the chart to help you. _____

Chairs		Stools	
Number of Chairs	Number of Leg Pieces	Number of Stools	Number of Leg Pieces
1	4	1	3
2	8	2	6
3		3	
4			

Use complete sentences to explain your thinking.
_____
_____

Solution

24. Three chairs need 12 leg pieces (3 X 4) and four stools need 12 leg pieces (4 X 3). Adding 12 plus 12 gives 24 leg pieces.
_____

3. If Mr. Sands had 29 leg pieces and he wants to use all of them. How many chairs and stools could he make? Give one possible answer (use the chart to help you). _____ Show your work.

Solution

One answer: 5 chairs and 3 stools. (5 X 4) + (3 X 3). (Also accept 0, 9; 1, 8; 2, 7; 3, 5; 4, 4; 6, 1; or 7, 0 as numbers of chairs and stools possible, respectively.)
_____

4. Someone said: "Mr. Sands only makes 4-legged chairs and stools because he doesn't know how to make anything else." Give the number of the sentence in the story that provides the best evidence to prove this person is wrong. _____

Use complete sentences to explain your thinking.
_____
_____

Solution

Sentence 11. In Sentence 11, we see that Mr. Sands can make tables and also rocking chairs, so he can make more furniture than just chairs.

Math Detective Certificate

Awarded to

_____

for _____

Signed _____

Date _____

Math Detective Certificate

Awarded to

_____

for _____

Date _____ Signed _____

I
NUMBER & NUMERATION

1—Latoya's Vacation

¹On August 4, Latoya looked at the calendar. ²She said, "Only two weeks and one day until my trip to New York City!" ³Latoya had never been to New York City. ⁴Her aunt was going to take her to the Statue of Liberty first, and then to a show on Broadway. ⁵Latoya was going to spend exactly one week in New York City. ⁶On the last Sunday before returning, she would visit her cousins in New Jersey for one day. ⁷Latoya would leave New York City on a Tuesday and return home that night. ⁸Latoya couldn't wait until her vacation!

August

Sun	Mon	Tues	Wed	Thurs	Fri	Sat
					1	2
3	4	5	6	7	8	9
10	11	12	13	14	15	16
17	18	19	20	21	22	23
24	25	26	27	28	29	30
31						

Questions

1. On which date does Latoya leave for her vacation? _____.

   Write the numbers of the two sentences that give the best evidence for your answer. _____, _____

2. If today is August 4th, how many more days until the day she leaves on vacation? _____

3. How many times has Latoya been to New York City?
   a. never
   b. once
   c. twice
   d. many times

   Write the number of the sentence that gives the best evidence for your answer. _____

4. In what order was Latoya going to visit the following places? Number her visits from the first to the third.

   _____ Broadway   _____ Her cousins   _____ The Statue of Liberty

5. On which date would Latoya visit her cousins in New Jersey? _____

   Write the number of the sentence that gives the best evidence for your answer. _____

6. On which date would Latoya return home?

   a. Tuesday, August 19th
   b. Tuesday, August 26th
   c. Monday, August 25th
   d. Monday, September 1st

7. Latoya's school starts on September 2. About how many days is it from the time Latoya gets home from New York City until she has to go back to school?

   a. About one day
   b. About seven days
   c. About three days
   d. About five days

8. Since it took only a day for Latoya to get home, where do you think Latoya lives? Explain your answer in complete sentences.

   a. She lives very close to New York City.
   b. She lives very far from New York City.
   c. She lives in New York City.
   d. I don't have enough information.

   _____
   _____
   _____

2—Eddy's Dog Shadow

[1]Eddy was very upset when his dog Shadow died. [2]Shadow was fourteen years old when he died. [3]Eddy's dad told him that most dogs, and most cats, live only about twelve years. [4]Eddy could not stop thinking about Shadow. [5]He looked up how long most pets live. [6]He made the list below. [7]Eddy wanted a new pet that would live a long time.

[8]After a few weeks, Eddy changed his mind about getting just another pet. [9]He asked his dad to buy him a new dog for his birthday. [10]Eddy thought, "It doesn't matter if my new dog doesn't live as long as I do. [11]What matters is that I will love my new dog just like I loved Shadow."

Life Spans of Some Pets	
Goldfish	10 years
Hamster	3 years
Horse	20 years
Rabbit	8 years
Snake	25 years
Turtle	35 years

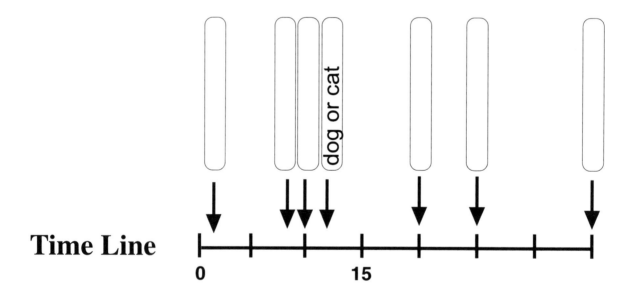

Time Line

Questions

1. a. Finish the number line above by adding the missing years.
   b. In the box above each arrow, write the name of the pet from Eddy's list that lives that number of years.

2. The words "life span" mean

    a. the length of time it takes to adopt a pet.
    b. the exact year when these pets will die.
    c. the day when Shadow died.
    d. about how long these pets live.

3. How much longer than a dog's normal life span did Shadow live?

   a. one year
   b. two years
   c. three years
   d. four years

   Write the numbers of the two sentences that give the best evidence for your answer. _____, _____

4. Which pet has a life span of about one-third that of a snake?

   a. turtle
   b. horse
   c. rabbit
   d. hamster

5. Which animal lives about half as long as a horse?

   a. goldfish
   b. hamster
   c. turtle
   d. snake

6. About how long do snakes live compared to dogs?

   a. about two times longer
   b. about half as long
   c. about the same
   d. about four times longer

7. Why do you think Eddie wanted a pet that would live a long time? Use complete sentences to explain your thinking.

   _____

   _____

8. Does the size of an animal have anything to do with how long it lives? _____ Name two animals on the timeline that support your answer. Use complete sentences to explain your thinking.

   _____

   _____

3—Who's Telling The Truth?

[1]Kim and her friends are playing a game with her younger brother, Sol. [2]"See if you can tell who's telling the truth!" she says.

[3]Tim says, "The product of 4 X 82 is less than 320. [4]Jing says, "The product of 8 X 31 is more than 240. [5]Lani says, "The quotient of 17 ÷ 4 is less than 4. [6]Jameel says, "The sum of 58 + 27 is more than the sum of 27 + 58." [7]Kim says, "The difference of 495 – 49 is less than the sum of 495 + 49."

[8]Sol listens very carefully. [9]"I don't think half of you are telling the truth!" he says.

Questions

1. *Product* means the answer to
    a. addition.
    b. subtraction.
    c. multiplication.
    d. division.

    Write the numbers of the two sentences that give the best evidence for your answer. _____, _____

2. A *sum* is what you find when doing
    a. addition.
    b. subtraction.
    c. multiplication.
    d. division.

    Write the numbers of the two sentences that give the best evidence for your answer. _____, _____

3. If you find a *difference*, you are doing
    a. addition.
    b. subtraction.
    c. multiplication.
    d. division.

    Write the number of the sentence that gives the best evidence for your answer. _____

MATH DETECTIVE Beginning   Number & Numeration

4. A *quotient* is the answer to

   a. addition.
   b. subtraction.
   c. multiplication.
   d. division.

   Write the number of the sentence that gives the best evidence for your answer. _____

5. 🚩 One way to figure out if Tim is telling the truth is to estimate the answer to 4 X 82. Since 4 X 80 is 320, then 4 X 82 must be bigger than 320. Estimate the answer to Jing's and Lani's problems to find out if they are telling the truth or not. Show your work here.

How I estimated Jing's problem	How I estimated Lani's problem

6. What is the fastest way to know if Jameel is telling the truth?

   a. by remembering that order doesn't matter when finding the sum
   b. by using a calculator to find both sums, and comparing the sums
   c. by adding both sums again and seeing if they are the same
   d. none of the above

7. How could Sol tell, without doing any arithmetic, if Kim is telling the truth? Use complete sentences to explain your thinking.

   _____

   _____

8. Who is telling the truth?

   a. Tim only
   b. Kim only
   c. Jameel and Lani
   d. Jing and Kim

4—School Supplies

¹Five students spent money for school supplies. ²Tom spent $21.00. ³The amount that John spent is a prime* number. ⁴The amount that Luis spent is a factor** of the number 24. ⁵Tina bought eight packages of markers for $6.00 each package. ⁶The number 10 is a factor of the amount that Mary spent.

*prime number: any whole number after 1 that has only two factors, one and itself

**factor: any number that goes into another number evenly, or without a remainder

TOM	$21.00
	$8.00
	$30.00
TINA	
	$17.00

Questions

Fill in the chart to help you answer the questions below.

1. What amount did John spend?

    a. $17.00
    b. $8.00
    c. $30.00
    d. $21.00

    Write the number of the sentence that gives the best evidence for your answer. _____

2. What amount did Luis spend?

    a. $21.00
    b. $8.00
    c. $17.00
    d. $30.00

    Write the number of the sentence that gives the best evidence for your answer. _____

MATH DETECTIVE Beginning   Number & Numeration

3. What amount did Mary spend?
   a. $17.00
   b. $8.00
   c. $30.00
   d. $21.00

   Write the number of the sentence that gives the best evidence for your answer. _____

4. How much more did Mary spend than Tom? _____ Show your work.

5. How much did all five students spend altogether? _____ Show your work.

6. 🎐 What are other factors, besides 10, for the amount that Mary spent?
   _____

5—At the Math Fair

¹At the Math Fair, you are allowed to throw two balls to try to knock out two numbers. ²If the sum of the two numbers is odd, you win a big stuffed animal. ³If the sum of the two numbers is even, you lose. ⁴Sammy said, "I'll try to hit the same odd number twice in a row. ⁵I think when you add two odd numbers you get an odd number all the time." ⁶George said, "No Sammy, you're wrong, because to get an odd number you have to hit two even numbers in a row!" ⁷Emma said, "Well, I think you're both wrong. ⁸To get an odd number you have to hit an even number and then an odd number or the other way around. ⁹I'm going to try to hit any number. ¹⁰If I hit an odd number on my first try, then I'll aim to hit an even number. ¹¹If I hit an even number on my first try, then I'll aim for an odd number." ¹²Sammy and George were not listening. ¹³They just continued to argue.

13	14	15
16	17	18
19	20	21

Questions

1. What does the word *sum* mean? Use a complete sentence to explain your thinking.
   _____
   _____

2. What happens if Sammy hits the number 17 and then the number 18?
   a. He loses.
   b. He gets to throw again.
   c. He wins.
   d. None of these.

3. On Emma's first try she hit the number 15. Next, she hopes to hit
   a. 15 again
   b. 18, 14, 16, or 20
   c. 13 or 17
   d. 20 but not 18

   Write the number of the sentence that gives the best evidence for your answer. _____

4. Sammy had a very good aim. He hit the number 17. Which of the following numbers would he hope to hit on his second try?
   a. 17 again.
   b. 20
   c. any even number
   d. any number

   Write the number of the sentence that gives the best evidence for your answer. _____

5. Is Sammy right when he says that the sum of two odd numbers is odd? _____ Show with an example why Sammy is right or wrong.

6. Is George right when he says that the sum of two even numbers is odd? _____ Show with an example why George is right or wrong.

Story, continued...

[14]At the end of the game, Emma hit the number 15 first and then she had very good aim and hit the number 20. [15]Sammy hit the number 17 twice in a row. [16]George hit the number 14. [17]He tried to aim for the number 20 but he hit 21 instead. [18]George was not unhappy after all!

7. Who won stuffed animals in this game?
   a. George
   b. Sammy
   c. Emma and George
   d. none of them

8. Circle the word *even* or *odd* to answer each question.

   a. The sum of two odd numbers is always   even   odd

   b. The sum of two even numbers is always   even   odd

   c. The sum of an odd number and an even number is always   even   odd

6—The Super Deli

¹Mei-jin, Lucy, and Sam went to the Super Deli. ²They each ordered one sandwich and one drink. ³Mei-jin, who does not like turkey, spent more money than Lucy. ⁴Lucy spent one more dollar than Sam. ⁵Sam does not like egg sandwiches. ⁶He had a soda with his sandwich. ⁷He spent about $3.00. ⁸One of them spent about $7.00.

⁹There was no tax on anything.

SANDWICHES		DRINKS	
Ham	$3.95	Soda	$1.10
Turkey	$4.75	Juice	$1.99
Chicken	$4.99	Coffee or Tea	$.80
Cheese	$1.95	Milk	$.90
Egg	$1.05		

Free fries with any sandwich!

Questions

1. What did Sam order? Estimate to find the answer.

    a. Ham sandwich and milk
    b. Ham sandwich and soda
    c. Cheese sandwich and soda
    d. Egg sandwich and soda

2. About how much money did Lucy spend? _____

    Write the numbers of the two sentences that give the best evidence for your answer. _____, _____

3. What sandwich and drink did Lucy have? Estimate to find the answer.

    a. Chicken sandwich and juice
    b. Ham sandwich and coffee
    c. Egg sandwich and milk
    d. Cheese sandwich and juice

4. Who spent about $7.00?

   a. Mei-jin
   b. Sam
   c. Lucy
   d. none of the above

5. What sandwich and drink did Mei-jin have? Estimate to find the answer.

   a. Turkey sandwich and soda
   b. Chicken sandwich and juice
   c. Turkey sandwich and juice
   d. Ham sandwich and tea

6. When Lucy's mother came to pick up Lucy at the deli, she ordered 6 ham sandwiches with fries and 5 juices to take home. Estimate how much she spent. Show your work.

7—The Party Favors

[1]Hannah is having three friends over for her birthday party. [2]Mrs. Li, Hannah's mother, wants to buy party favors for Hannah's friends. [3]Mrs. Li wanted each of Hannah's friends to get the same number of party favors and have only one left over for Hannah's little brother. [4]Hannah made a chart of how many party favors each of her friends would get if Mrs. Li bought between 18 and 26 party favors. [5]Mrs. Li can spend no more than $12 on party favors.

Questions

1. How many girls are coming to Hannah's party including Hannah? _____

   Write the number of the sentence that gives the best evidence for your answer. _____

2. Which is NOT important to Mrs. Li?

   a. Hannah's brother has as many favors as everyone else
   b. Hannah's brother gets at least one favor
   c. party favors cost no more than $12
   d. each girl gets the same number of favors

   Write the number of the sentence that gives the best evidence for your answer. _____

3. If Mrs. Li buys 24 party favors, what should she do to find how many party favors each friend gets (if she does not worry about Hannah's little brother or Hannah)?

   a. Divide 24 by 3
   b. Divide 3 by 24
   c. Multiply 3 times 24
   d. None of the above

4. Complete the table below to show how many party favors each friend would get. Don't worry about Hannah's little brother when you do the chart.

Party Favors	Favors ÷ 3 (Number each friend gets)	Remainder
25		
24		
23		
22		
21		
20		
19		

5. Without doing any arithmetic (look at your completed chart), what would the remainder be for 26 party favors? _____ What would the remainder be for 18 party favors? _____

6. Use one or two examples from the chart above to show that this pattern is true: Every multiple of three when divided by three has a remainder of zero.

_____

7. When dividing by 3, what are the only possible remainders?

_____

8—The Five Wealthy Women

¹Five women who were friends won the state lottery. ²They got to split the total amount evenly after taxes. ³During a period of two weeks, they each came to the City Bank to put money in their bank accounts. ⁴On Monday, Anna put seven million dollars in her account. ⁵Two days later, Antonia put seven hundred thousand dollars in her account. ⁶Then the day after, Andrea put in seventy thousand seven hundred dollars. ⁷Exactly a week after Andrea came to the bank, Ali put seventy thousand seventy dollars in her account. ⁸The next day, Abby put seven million seven hundred seventy dollars in her account. ⁹Abby was the only one who put everything she won into the bank.

Questions

1. How much money did Anna put in the bank?

    a. $700,000
    b. $7,000,000
    c. $70,000,000
    d. none of the above

    Write the number of the sentence that gives the best evidence for your answer. _____

2. On which day did Antonia go to the bank? _____

    Write the numbers of the two sentences that give the best evidence for your answer. _____, _____.

3. How much money did Antonia put in the bank?

    a. $70,000,000
    b. $7,000,000
    c. $7,700,700
    d. $700,000

    Write the number of the sentence that gives the best evidence for your answer. _____

MATH DETECTIVE Beginning Number & Numeration

4. On what day did Andrea put money in the bank? _____

5. How much money did Andrea put in the bank? _____ (write it as a numeral).

6. How much money did Ali put in the bank? _____ (write it as a numeral).

7. On which day did Abby go to the bank? _____

8. How much money did Abby put in the bank?
   a. $7,700,070
   b. $7,770,000
   c. $7,000,770
   d. $ 770,070

9. What was the total amount of lottery money before it was split among all five friends? _____ Show your work.

10. Make a list of the amounts of money that were put in the bank, from least to greatest. Beside each, write the name of the wealthy woman and the day of the week that amount was put into the bank. Then find the total amount that was put into the bank.

Day of the week	Name	Amount put in the bank
_____	_____	$ _____
_____	_____	$ _____
_____	_____	$ _____
_____	_____	$ _____
_____	_____	$ _____
	Total	_____

9—Leafy Lengths

[1]Luis and Amy had to make a leaf scrapbook for science class. [2]They measured some leaves with their centimeter ruler. [3]Amy found the three biggest leaves. [4]Luis found the three smallest leaves.

Questions

1. Graph the lengths of the leaves they found by placing the letters on the number line. The first one has been done for you.

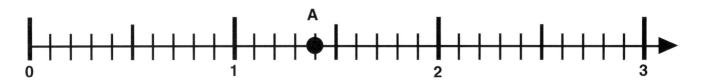

2. The leaves found are listed by letter at the right. Write the letters of Luis's leaves in order from smallest to largest.

   _____, _____, _____

   Write the number of the sentence that gives the best evidence for your answer. _____

Leaf Lengths

A	1.4	cm (already on the graph)
B	2.3	cm
C	.8	cm
D	.5	cm
E	2.05	cm
F	1.7	cm

3. Write the letters of the Amy's leaves in order from smallest to largest.

   _____, _____, _____

   Write the number of the sentence that gives the best evidence for your answer. _____

II
PATTERNS

10—The Family Tree

[1]All over the world, many families keep records of their ancestors. [2]Ancestors are family members that came before your parents, like your grandparents, great-grandparents, etc. [3]Tammy asked Grandma Emma to help her make a family tree. [4]With her grandmother's help, Tammy was lucky enough to get the names of three generations of her family. [5]A generation is a set of people about the same age.

[6]Tammy's parents are Teresa and Andy. [7]Teresa's mother and father are called Emma and Joe.

[8]Joe's parents were called Mary and Tom. [9]Emma's mother and father were called Sofía and Antonio. [10]They died when Tammy was a little girl.

[11]Andy's parents are Angela and Camilo. [12]Angela's mother was named Ana. [13]Angela's father is still alive and they call him Great Grampa Mario. [14]Camilo's mother was Elena, and Camilo's father was named Peter.

Questions

1. Finish Tammy's family tree:

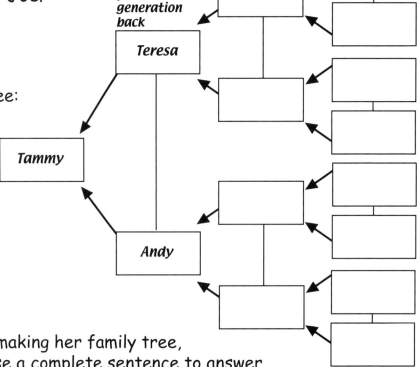

2. Did Tammy get any help making her family tree, and if so, from whom? Use a complete sentence to answer.

_____

_____

Write the numbers of the two sentences that give the best evidence for your answer. _____, _____

MATH DETECTIVE Beginning   Patterns

3. How many generations, not counting Tammy's generation, are shown on the family tree? _____

4. Who died when Tammy was a little girl? _____

   Write the numbers of the two sentences that give the best evidence for your answer. _____, _____

5. Which of Tammy's great-grandparents do you know for sure is still living?

   _____

   Write the number of the sentence that gives the best evidence for your answer. _____

6. Who were Teresa's grandparents on her father's side?

   _____

7. Who is Ana's and Mario's grandchild? _____

8. Continue to fill out the chart below.

Tammy	1 generation back Tammy's parents	2 generations back Tammy's Grandparents	3 generations back Tammy's Great Grandparents	4 generations back etc.	5 generations back etc.
1	2	4	___	___	___

   Describe the pattern, using a complete sentence.

   _____

   _____

9. Tammy found one picture of each of the people in the chart above, starting with herself and going back five generations. How many pictures did she find? _____ Show your work.

11—Trip to the Theater

¹A theater has ten rows. ²The first row has six seats. ³Each row after that has two more seats than the row in front of it. ⁴Ms. Kamen wants to take her class to the theater. ⁵She would like to sit with her seventeen students all in one row. ⁶She would prefer not to have any other people sitting in the same row as her class. ⁷The theater charges $5.00 for each adult and $2.00 for each child.

Questions

1. Use the grid below to finish drawing the number of seats in the theater. Continue the pattern that has been started.

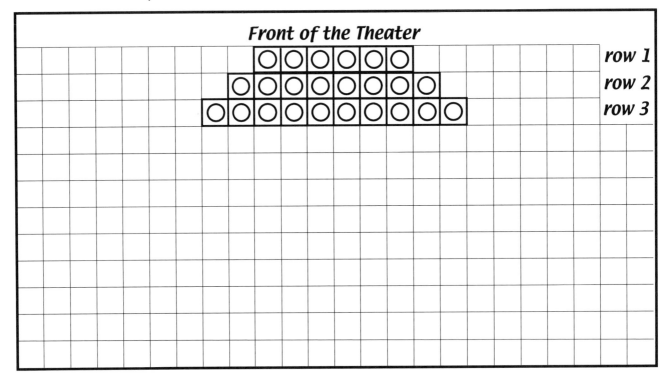

2. How many seats does Ms. Kamen need for herself and her class? _____

   Write the number of the sentence that gives the best evidence for your answer. _____

3. How many seats are in row 5? _____

   Write the number of the sentence that gives the best evidence for your answer. _____

4. Some students from another school wanted to sit with Ms. Kamen's class. Would Ms. Kamen be happy with that? _____

   Write the number of the sentence that gives the best evidence for your answer. _____

5. Which row do you think Ms. Kamen should reserve for herself and her class? _____ Use complete sentences to explain your thinking.

   _____

   _____

6. Which sentence tells you how much it costs to get into the theater? _____

   What did Ms. Kamen have to pay for herself and her seventeen students? _____. Show your work.

7. Use a calculator to find the total number of seats in the theater. Show your work.

8. When the theater was full, there were 40 adults and the rest were children. How much money did the theater make on that day? _____ Show your work.

12—The Toy Factory

¹At a toy factory, it takes the same amount of time to create the jumper on a teddy bear as it does to create the suit of an action hero. ²A teddy bear's jumper takes three buttons. ³An action hero's outfit takes five buttons. ⁴After today's work, the owner of the toy factory wanted to know how many teddy bears and action heroes had been made. ⁵However, a truck had already taken the teddy bears and the action heroes to the store. ⁶No one could remember how many were made.

⁷One of the factory workers said, "I know that we had 100 buttons today when we started, and now we have only 36 buttons left." ⁸The owner said, "If no teddy bears lost their button, like Corduroy did in that famous story, and no action hero lost buttons either, then I think we can figure this out!"

Questions

1. Fill out the chart below to help you figure out how many teddy bears and action heroes were made today.

Number of Each Figure	Buttons for Teddy Bears	Buttons for Action Heroes	Total Buttons
1	3	5	8
2	6	10	

MATH DETECTIVE Beginning   Patterns

2. How many buttons altogether are needed for one teddy bear and one action hero? _____.

    Write the numbers of the two sentences that give the best evidence for your answer. _____, _____

3. If it took 30 minutes to make a teddy bear jumper, how much time would it take to make an action hero suit?_____

    Write the number of the sentence that gives the best evidence for your answer. _____

4. How many buttons altogether were used to make teddy bears and action heroes today? _____ Show your work.

    Write the number of the sentence that gives the best evidence for your answer. _____

5. How many teddy bears and action heroes were made today?

    a. 8 teddy bears and 8 action heroes
    b. 4 teddy bears and 4 action heroes
    c. 10 teddy bears and 10 action heroes
    d. 5 teddy bears and 5 action heroes

6. 🚩 If 40 buttons in total were used another day, how many teddy bears and action heroes were made on that day? Assume equal time is spent on bears and heroes. _____ Use complete sentences to explain your thinking.

    _____
    _____
    _____

13—The 35¢ Yummy Bar

¹A Yummy Bar costs 35 cents. ²The machine takes only exact change and does not take pennies. ³Maria and her five friends each wanted a Yummy Bar. ⁴They each had exactly 35 cents to put in the machine, but no one had the same number of coins! ⁵Maria had seven coins. ⁶Louisa had six coins. ⁷Melissa had 5 coins. ⁸Kevin had two fewer coins than Louisa. ⁹Sue had three coins. ¹⁰Dave had half as many coins as Kevin.

Questions

1. Who had the most coins? _____. How many coins did she have? _____

   Write the number of the sentence that gives the best evidence for your answer. _____

2. How many coins did Kevin have? _____.

   Write the numbers of the two sentences that give the best evidence for your answer. _____, _____

3. How many coins did Dave have? _____.

4. What kind of coins can the machine take? Use complete sentences to explain your thinking.

   _____

   _____

   Write the numbers of the two sentences that give the best evidence for your answer. _____, _____

5. On the next page, complete the chart to help you find what types of coins each friend had.

The 35¢ Yummy Bar

Name	Number of Coins	Type of Coins	Total
Maria	7	⑤ + ⑤ + ⑤ + ⑤ + ⑤ + ⑤ + ⑤	= 35¢
Louisa			= 35¢
Melissa			= 35¢
Kevin			= 35¢
Sue			= 35¢
Dave			= 35¢

III
OPERATIONS

14—The City Bus

¹A city bus has 50 passenger seats. ²No one may stand while the bus is running. ³The bus starts out empty and, at the first stop, picks up forty people. ⁴On the second stop, fifteen people get off and no one gets on. ⁵At the third stop, the bus picks up ten more people and three people get off. ⁶At the fourth stop, no one gets off, but twenty-three people are waiting to get on. ⁷Is there enough room for all twenty-three people? ⁸The bus continues without any more stops until it gets to the zoo.

Complete the chart on the next page as you answer the questions.

Questions

1. Where is the city bus going?

    a. to the school
    b. to the park
    c. to the zoo
    d. downtown

    Write the number of the sentence that gives the best evidence for your answer. _____

2. Would the bus driver allow some people to stand if the bus got full? _____

    Write the number of the sentence that gives the best evidence for your answer. _____

3. How many empty seats are left on the bus right after the first stop? _____

    Write the numbers of the two sentences that give the best evidence for your answer. _____, _____

4. How many people are on the bus right after the second stop? _____

    Write the numbers of the two sentences that give the best evidence for your answer. _____, _____

5. How many seats are empty right after the second stop? _____ Show your work.

6. How many seats are left empty right after the third stop? _____ Show your work.

7. a. Are there enough seats left on the bus for twenty-three people when the bus makes its fourth stop? _____. Use complete sentences to explain your thinking.

   _____

   _____

   b. Complete the chart to show the correct numbers. Try to fit as many people as possible of the 23 people who want to get on at the fourth stop.

STOP #	Passengers that Get On	Passengers that Get Off	Passengers On the Bus	Empty Seats
One				
Two				
Three				
Four				

15—Eddy's Achy Ride

¹Eddy had to help his stepmom sell her famous jumbo cookies around the neighborhood.

²Eddy left his house and rode his bike to Kiki's house. ³Kiki bought 5 cookies.

⁴On the way to Frankie's house, Eddy got very hungry. ⁵He ate half a dozen, or 6, cookies. ⁶He knew he shouldn't be eating cookies. ⁷Frankie was home and bought twice as many cookies as Kiki bought.

⁸Eddy was still hungry, so on the way to Emma's house he ate a dozen cookies. ⁹Emma's dad bought twice as many cookies as Frankie bought. ¹⁰Eddy looked at the bag of cookies. ¹¹There were plenty of cookies left.

¹²He stopped at Terri's house, but she was not there. ¹³There was a sign on her door that read, "I've gone to the park to write."

¹⁴Eddy went to the park, and Terri bought twice as many cookies as Emma's dad bought. ¹⁵While at the park, Eddy ate a third of a dozen cookies. ¹⁶It was time to return home.

¹⁷When Eddy got home, his friends were waiting outside to play with him. ¹⁸He wasn't feeling so good. ¹⁹He had to go to his room! ²⁰In the bag, there were only three cookies left. ²¹Eddy had only $75.00 in cookie money. ²²How many cookies did Eddy start out with?

Questions

1. How many cookies is a dozen cookies? _____.

   Write the number of the sentence that gives the best evidence for your answer. _____

2. How many cookies is two dozen cookies? _____

3. How many cookies is a third of a dozen cookies? _____ Show your work.

MATH DETECTIVE Beginning   Operations

4. Complete this chart to help you find how many cookies Eddy sold and ate!

Cookies Sold	
At Kiki's	5
At Frankie's	
At Emma's	
At the park	
Total	

Cookies Eaten	
On the way to Kiki's	0
On the way to Frankie's	6
On the way to Emma's	
At the park	
Total	

5. How many cookies did Eddy start out with? _____ Show your work. Use your completed charts to help you.

6. 🎉 How much did each cookie cost? _____ Show your work.

7. What is the most likely reason why Eddy had to go to his room when he got home?

   a. Eddy felt sick.
   b. Eddy was rewarded for eating the cookies.
   c. Eddy's friends did not want to play with him.
   d. None of the above.

16—An Apple a Day

[1]Ms. Kamen asked her class to watch the foods they ate. [2]She said, "The next time you eat potato chips, I want you to count how many potato chips you eat!" [3]She cut out the nutrition facts from a bag of potato chips and showed this to the class:

Nutrition Facts

One serving: 15 chips

Amount per serving:

Calories—150

Total Fat—10 grams

[4]The next day, the class made a chart of the numbers of potato chips that Eddy, Zoe, and Tyler ate at lunch time. [5]The number of potato chips that Zoe and Tyler ate is shown on the chart below. [6]Eddy loves potato chips. [7]He had twice, or two times, the number of servings that Tyler had. [8]Help Ms. Kamen finish the chart below. [9]Ms. Kamen told her class, "The next time you feel hungry, go eat an apple. [10]An apple has only 66 calories and has less than 1 gram of fat! [11]An apple a day...well, you know how the saying goes."

Name	Servings	Number of chips	Grams of fat	Calories
Zoe	1	15		
Tyler	2			
Eddy				

Questions

Complete the chart as you answer the questions, using the nutrition facts and the evidence in the text.

1. How many chips did Tyler eat?
    a. 15 chips
    b. 30 chips
    c. 45 chips
    d. 60 chips

2. How many grams of fat did Tyler eat?

   a. 10 grams
   b. 20 grams
   c. 30 grams
   d. 40 grams

3. How many chips did Eddy eat?

   a. 15 chips
   b. 30 chips
   c. 45 chips
   d. 60 chips

4. How many grams of fat did Eddy eat?

   a. 10 grams
   b. 20 grams
   c. 30 grams
   d. 40 grams

5. How many more calories did Eddy eat than did Tyler? _____ Show your work.

6. How many more calories are there in one serving of chips than in one apple? _____ Show your work.

7. Why do you think Ms. Kamen wants her class to know about the nutritional facts of potato chips? Use complete sentences to explain your thinking.

   _____

   _____

17—Time to Buy a New Clock

¹Dave wants to buy a new clock for his mother's birthday. ²He finds two clocks that he likes. ³One clock is round and green, and the other clock is square and blue. ⁴He knows that green and blue are his mom's favorite colors. ⁵The green clock uses an electric cord and costs $21.99. ⁶The blue clock works with one battery, but the battery is not included. ⁷It costs $17.50 for the blue clock. ⁸Dave finds out that one battery costs $2.79. ⁹Dave has $25.00. ¹⁰He would like to have some money left over to buy wrapping paper. ¹¹Dave lives in a state where there is no sales tax.

 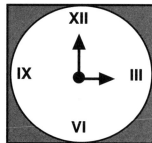

Questions

1. How much does the green clock cost? _____

   Write the number of the sentence that gives the best evidence for your answer. _____

2. How much will Dave pay for the blue clock and one battery? _____
   Show your work.

   Write the numbers of the two sentences that give the best evidence for your answer. _____, _____

3. Which clock is more expensive? _____ Use complete sentences to explain your thinking.

   _____

   _____

4. Which of the following do you agree with after reading the story?

   a. Dave's mom prefers red clocks.
   b. All green clocks require batteries.
   c. Dave has more than $20.00
   d. Dave's mom prefers clocks with Roman numerals.

   Write the number of the sentence that gives the best evidence for your answer. _____

5. What else does Dave want to buy? _____

   Write the number of the sentence that gives the best evidence for your answer. _____

6. Wrapping paper costs $4.00 a roll. Would Dave have enough money left over to buy wrapping paper if he buys the blue clock? _____ What if he buys the green clock? _____ Use complete sentences to explain your thinking.

   _____

   _____

7. Does Dave need to pay sales tax? _____

   Write the number of the sentence that gives the best evidence for your answer. _____

8. If Dave has to buy one more battery (at the same price as the first) after the first one runs out, which clock do you think is the better buy? Use complete sentences to explain your thinking.

   _____

   _____

MATH DETECTIVE Beginning   Operations

18—The Toy Sale

¹Emily's mom is having a garage sale. ²Emily made a poster of the toys her mom is going to sell. ³Emily will sell the tractor only to her friend Marcos.

Toy Sale Prices	
Box of Puzzles	$ 14.00
Bike	$ 54.00
Tractor	$ 13.00
Ice Skates	$ 23.00
Wagon	$ 7.00
Video Game	$ 17.00
Box of Board Games	$ 6.00

Questions

1. John arrived at the sale first and spent exactly $20.00 on two toys. What toys did he buy?

    a. tractor and wagon
    b. box of puzzles and box of board games
    c. ice skates and wagon
    d. box of puzzles and wagon

    Write the number of the sentence that helps you decide on the best answer.
    _____

2. Luis arrived next and bought one toy. He paid with a $20 bill and got $3.00 back. What toy did he buy? Use complete sentences to explain your thinking.

    _____

    _____

3. Marcos came to the sale after Luis. He bought two toys and spent exactly $20. What did he buy?

    a. tractor and wagon
    b. box of puzzles and box of board games
    c. ice skates and wagon
    d. box of puzzles and wagon

4. Tina bought the ice skates and paid with a $50 bill. How much change did she get back? _____ Show your work.

5. Tommy wanted to buy the bike, but his mom thought the bike was too expensive. Emma's mom sold Tommy the bike for $8.00 less. Tommy's mom paid with a $100 bill. How much change did his mom get back? _____ Show your work in two steps.

    New Price of the Bike   Change from $100

6. At the end of the sale, all the toys were sold and you want to add up the sales without a calculator. What shortcut could you use to group and add the amounts of the toys that were sold, not including the bike? Show your work.

19—Dinner with Ramón

¹Omar and his older brother Ramón went out to dinner at La Casita Restaurant. ²When they sat down, the waitress told them that the chicken dinner was $2.00 cheaper than the price on the menu. ³Omar had the chicken with rice dish and one piece of apple pie. ⁴Ramón had the steak and one serving of flan.

LA CASITA MENU

Arroz con Pollo (Chicken with Rice)	$9.50	Flan (Custard)	$2.50
Bistec (Steak)	$13.50	Cake	$3.00
Bean Burritos	$ 5.00	Apple Pie	$3.20

All dinners served with salad

Questions

1. What is the new price of the chicken with rice dish? _____ Show your work.

   Write the number of the sentence that gives the best evidence for your answer. _____

2. How much did Omar's dinner cost, including his dessert? _____ Show your work.

   Write the number of the sentence that gives the best evidence for your answer. _____

3. How much did Ramón's dinner cost, including his dessert? Show your work.

Write the number of the sentence that gives the best evidence for your answer. _____

4. Apple pie costs how much more than flan? _____ Show your work.

5. The waitress gave Ramón this check for both dinners. Ramón saw that the waitress made a mistake. Finish the check and correct the mistake below. Then find the total. Do not worry about tip or tax.

La Casita

Arroz con pollo	$_____.___
Bistec	$_____.___
Apple pie	$ 3.20
Flan	$ 4.50
Total	$_____.___

Thank you...
Please come again!

20—Mr. Papas at the Toy Store

[1]Mr. Papas works at a toy store. [2]Here is a chart of the hours he worked during one week. [3]Mr. Papas makes $10 an hour.

Week of October 2–6

Day	A.M. Time Worked	Total Hours	Day	P.M. Time Worked	Total Hours
Mon.	6:30–Noon	5 1/2	Mon.	12:30–4:00	
Tues.	7:30–Noon		Tues.	1:00–5:30	
Wed.	7:00–Noon		Wed.	1:00–5:30	
Thurs.	6:30–Noon		Thurs.	1:00–4:30	
Fri.	8:30–Noon		Fri.	12:30–3:00	
	Total			Total	

Total hours for the week _____

Questions

1. Complete the chart above as you answer the questions below.

2. How many hours did Mr. Papas work on Monday, October 2? _____. Show your work.

3. On which day did he work the most hours? _____ How many hours altogether did he work that day? _____. Show your work.

4. Mr. Papas gets a lunch break at noon. Does he take the same length of time for his lunch break each day? _____. Use complete sentences to explain your thinking.

_____

_____

5. How many hours altogether did Mr. Papas work during the week of October 2-6? _____ Show your work.

6. How much money did he make the week of October 2-6? _____ Show your work.

Write the number of the sentence that gives the best evidence for your answer. _____

7. Another week, Mr. Papas made $360. How many hours did he work that week? _____ Show your work.

8. 🚩 In most jobs, if a person works over 40 hours, he gets paid more per hour for all the hours he works over 40 hours (this is called overtime hours). How many hours over the 40 hours did Mr. Papas work during the week of October 2-6? _____.

9. 🚩 If Mr. Papas got paid twice as much per hour for his overtime hours, how much money would he make altogether for the week of October 2-6? _____. Show your work.

IV
GEOMETRY

21—Off to the State Fair

[1]Mary was from a small town and she had never been to a state fair. [2]When she visited her friend Lucy over the summer, Lucy's parents took them to the state fair. [3]When they arrived at the fair, the first thing they did was visit the information booth. [4]At the information booth they learned that they had to walk along the paths shown by the grid below. [5]They were also given a schedule of events and a map.

[6]At the end of the day, Mary couldn't believe how many people work all year to get ready for the state fair. [7]She also loved the animal shows and all the international food she got to taste.

[8]The numbers (1, 4) shown beside Animal Show make up what is known as an ordered pair. [9]They show this event's location on the grid. [10]To find it, start at 0, go over 1 unit to the right, then up 4 units.

Questions

1. a. On the list, label each attraction with the ordered pair showing its location. The first one is done for you. (The list is not in the order in which the family made stops.)

   A Animal Show   (1, 4)
   B Information Booth   _____
   C Restaurant   _____
   D Restrooms   _____
   E Games Area   _____
   F International Food   _____
      & Candy
   G New Tools   _____

   b. Find and label each point on the map.

   H The Music Stage   (9, 2)
   I Crafts Building   (4, 0)
   J Face Painting   (0, 7)
   K Rides   (9, 5)

2. Explain what you do to graph the ordered pair (9, 2).
   _____
   _____

   Write the number of the sentence that gives the best evidence for your answer. _____

3. From the Restaurant, the Information Booth is _____ units away.

4. From the New Tools Building, the International Food & Candy Building is _____ units away.

5. 🚩 Lucy's dad wanted to walk from the Restrooms to the New Tools Building. What is the least number of units he can walk to get there? _____ Be careful! There is a pond in the middle!

6. Where was Lucy's dad when he was told that he had to follow the paths shown on the grid? _____.

   Write the number of the sentence that gives the best evidence for your answer. _____

22—Luis's Letter

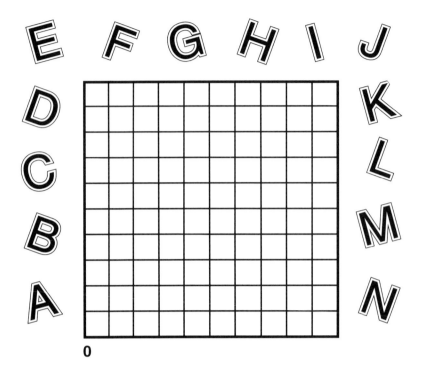

¹Ms. Kamen told her students to graph the first letter of their name on a grid like the one above. ²Luis graphed the first letter of his name. ³He connected the points graphed from these ordered pairs in this sequence: A (2,2); B (6,2); C (6,4); D (4,4); E (4,7); F (2,7); and back to A (2,2).

⁴Ms. Kamen wanted her students to find out if the perimeter of their letter was the same as the area inside their letter. ⁵Ms. Kamen reminded Luis that to find the perimeter he had to count all the units around the outside of his letter. ⁶Ms. Kamen also told Luis that to find the area he had to count all the squares inside his letter. ⁷Luis said, "I don't need to do both, Ms. Kamen. ⁸The perimeter of my letter must be the same as the area of my letter."

Questions

1. Plot and connect the points that Luis graphed. Don't forget to label each point.

   Write the numbers of the two sentences that help you identify what letter you should have graphed. _____, _____

2. What is the distance from point A to point B? _____

3. What is the perimeter of Luis's letter? _____ Use complete sentences to explain how you found the perimeter of Luis's letter.

_____

_____

4. Find the area of Luis's letter. _____ Show your work.

Write the number of the sentence that gives the best evidence for your answer. _____

5. Was Luis correct when he said that the perimeter of his letter was the same as the area of his letter? _____ Use complete sentences to explain your thinking.

_____

_____

23—Annie's Angles Report

[1]It was time for the end-of-the-year geometry reports. [2]Annie had to give a report on angles for her class. [3]She began, "What would life be like without angles? [4]Can you imagine a world without straight lines? [5]We would all be going around in circles!" [6]Ms. Kamen, her teacher, tried not to laugh. [7]Annie continued, "Two line segments, or rays, joined at one corner make an angle. [8]Angles are measured in degrees. [9]An angle less than 90 degrees is called an acute angle. [10]You can remember 'cute and little.'" [11]Annie showed this poster:

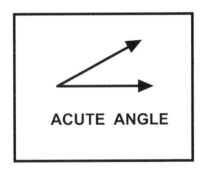

ACUTE ANGLE

[12]"A right angle, or perfect corner, is exactly 90 degrees." [13]Annie showed this poster:

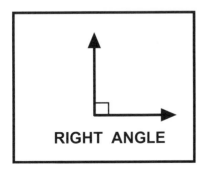

RIGHT ANGLE

[14]Annie then said, "An angle that is more than 90 degrees but less than 180 degrees is called an obtuse angle." [15]Annie showed the poster below. [16]Annie said, "My favorite obtuse angle is the angle the clock makes at 2:35 when it's time to go home!" [17]Everyone laughed, even Ms. Kamen.

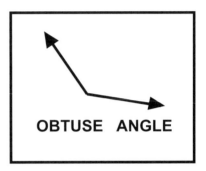

OBTUSE ANGLE

[18]Annie continued, "A straight line is 180 degrees. [19]That is because two right angles next to each other make a straight line." [20]Annie's last poster looked like this:

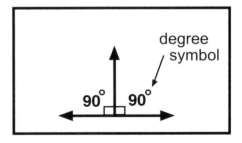

[21]Annie asked, "Any questions?"

[22]Ms. Kamen asked, "Does anyone now know how many degrees are in a circle?" [23]Luis said 360° and Maya said 270°. [24]Ms. Kamen thanked Annie and the class clapped.

MATH DETECTIVE Beginning

Geometry

Questions

1. What units do we use to compare the sizes of different angles?

   a. inches
   b. degrees
   c. centimeters
   d. meters

   Write the number of the sentence that gives the best evidence for your answer. _____

2. What do you call a 120-degree angle?

   a. acute
   b. right
   c. obtuse
   d. straight

   Write the number of the sentence that gives the best evidence for your answer. _____

3. What do you call an angle that is 25 degrees? _____

   Write the number of the sentence that gives the best evidence for your answer. _____

4. How many degrees are in one corner of this rectangle? _____

5. Why is the angle of a straight line 180°? Use complete sentences to explain your thinking. _____
   _____

6. On the clock, draw the time that Annie calls her favorite obtuse angle.

7. 🎉 Who had the right answer to Ms. Kamen's question in sentence 22, Luis or Maya? _____ Use complete sentences to explain.
   _____
   _____

© 2003 Critical Thinking Books & Software • www.CriticalThinking.com • 800-458-4849

24—Trip to the Skating Rink

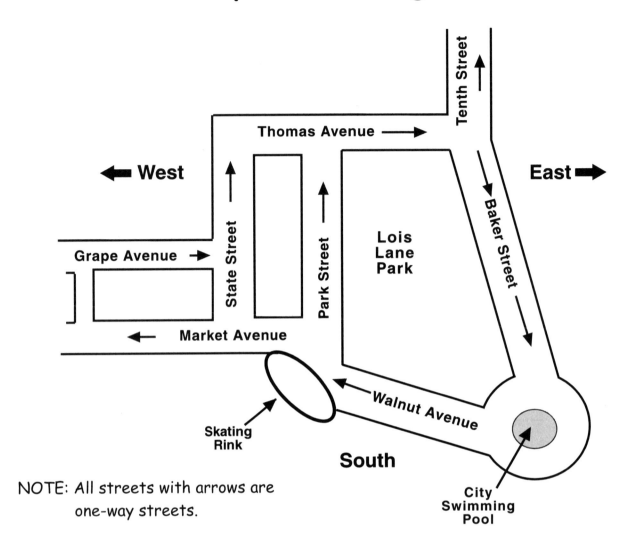

NOTE: All streets with arrows are one-way streets.

¹The Ross family lives on Market Avenue. ²On the way to the skating rink, Julia Ross and her mom are going to pick up some of Julia's friends. ³Lucy lives on Grape Avenue. ⁴Tony lives on State Street and Helen lives on Baker Street. ⁵Mrs. Ross also has to pick up Julia's older brother at the City Swimming Pool. ⁶He also wants to go to the skating rink. ⁷Mrs. Ross does not mind picking up all the children. ⁸She loves to drive around Lois Lane Park anyway.

Questions

1. On what street does Julia live? _____

   Write the numbers of the two sentences that give the best evidence for your answer. _____, _____

2. Which of Julia's friends lives on a street that runs parallel (side by side) to Julia's street? _____

3. Which of Julia's friends lives on a street that makes a perfect corner (right angle) with Market Avenue?_____

   Write the number of the sentence that gives the best evidence for your answer. _____

4. Which street makes a perfect corner (right angle) with Park Street? _____

5. What kind of angle does Thomas Avenue make with the street that Helen lives on?

   a. right angle
   b. acute angle
   c. obtuse angle
   d. straight angle

6. What kind of angle does Baker Street make with Walnut Avenue at the City Swimming Pool?

   a. right angle
   b. straight angle
   c. obtuse angle
   d. acute angle

7. List all the streets on the map that are parallel to Market Avenue.

   _____

8. List all the streets on the map that are parallel to State Street.

   _____

9. To get to the skating rink, why does Mrs. Ross need to drive around Lois Lane Park? Use complete sentences to explain your thinking.

   _____
   _____

25—The Pastry Shop

¹A new pastry shop opened up in the center of town. ²Every pastry has a different shape. ³Ice cream is sold only in cones. ⁴Cakes are sold only in the shape of a cube. ⁵Candy is sold only in small spheres of different colors. ⁶Chocolate fudge is sold only in the shape of a pyramid. ⁷Brown bread is sold only in the shape of cylinders.

⁸Tammy, Eddy, Ada, Lucy, and Melissa went to the pastry shop one Saturday afternoon. ⁹The lady at the pastry shop said, "Pick your dessert according to the shape you like best. ¹⁰All my desserts are wonderful!"

¹¹Eddy said, "I love basketball, so I'll pick ten of those candies." ¹²Lucy said, "My favorite shape is a party hat because today is my birthday, so I'll take an ice cream cone." ¹³The lady at the store gave her a free ice cream. ¹⁴Tammy said, "I love the shape of triangles, so I'll pick one chocolate fudge." ¹⁵Ada said, "I'll just get one of those brown breads shaped like little cans for my grandmother." ¹⁶Melissa said, "I don't think I have a favorite shape, so I'll just take one of those small cakes shaped like a little block."

Questions

1. Which shape has a face, or side, with a triangle on it?

    a. cone
    b. pyramid
    c. sphere
    d. circle

    Write the numbers of the two sentences that give the best evidence for your answer. _____, _____

MATH DETECTIVE Beginning   Geometry

2. Which object is a "sphere"?

   a. a TV
   b. a basketball
   c. a shoe box
   d. a pencil

   Write the numbers of the two sentences that give the best evidence for your answer. _____, _____

3. Who bought the "cube"? _____

   Write the numbers of the two sentences that give the best evidence for your answer. _____, _____

4. What is a "cone" shaped like?

   a. party hat
   b. a ball
   c. a scoop of ice cream.
   d. none of the above

   Write the number of the sentence that gives the best evidence for your answer. _____

5. What geometry shape is like a "can"?

   a. sphere
   b. a cube
   c. a cone
   d. a cylinder

   Write the numbers of the two sentences that give the best evidence for your answer. _____, _____

6. Complete the chart that appears on the next page.

MATH DETECTIVE Beginning — Geometry

Directions: Based on the story, write the geometry name for the object, the name of the dessert that had that shape, and who bought the dessert.

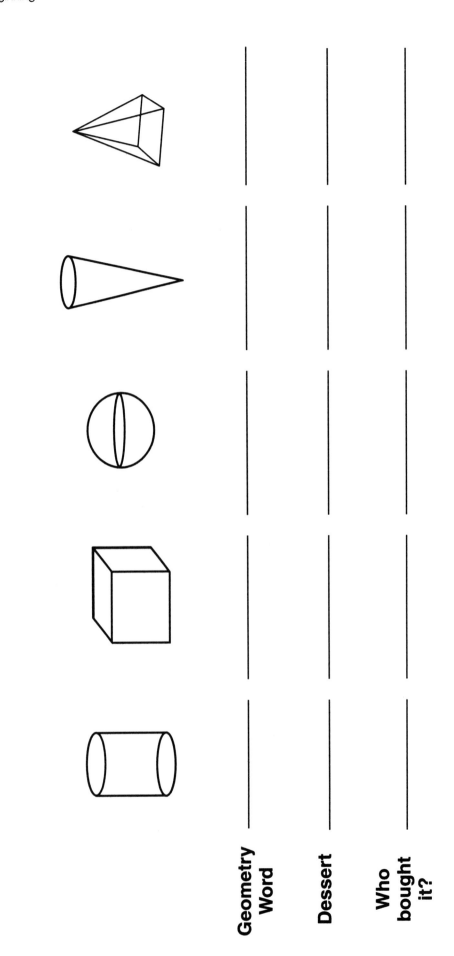

Geometry Word

Dessert

Who bought it?

26—Geometry Art

¹Emily and Amanda were making designs with polygon* pieces. ²Amanda found a chart in her math book with the names of some polygons and the number of sides for each one. ³Amanda started to copy the chart, but she did not finish. ⁴When Emily saw the chart she said, "Amanda, you did not finish the chart." ⁵Emily said, "I know that a nine-sided polygon is called a nonagon." ⁶Emily's dad, who was sitting in the living room, heard the conversation and said, "And a ten-sided polygon is called a decagon. ⁷You can remember the word 'decade,' which means every ten years." ⁸Emily said, "Thanks, Dad!"

⁹Later, Emily made a design with only six-sided polygons. ¹⁰Amanda's design was made by using only eight-sided and three-sided polygons.

*A polygon is a many-sided shape.

Questions

1. Finish Emily's chart at the right.

2. What is the name of the polygon that Emily is using for her design?
   a. quadrilateral
   b. pentagon
   c. hexagon
   d. nonagon

3. Which geometry shape is Amanda NOT using for her design?
   a. triangle
   b. octagon
   c. polygon
   d. pentagon

Polygon Name	Number of Sides
triangle	3 sides
quadrilateral	4 sides
pentagon	5 sides
hexagon	6 sides
heptagon	7 sides
octagon	8 sides
nonagon	
	10 sides

4. Below each design, write the name of the girl who made it.

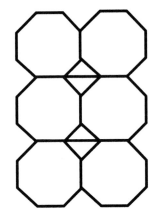

This design was made by

_____

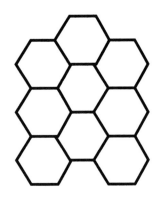

This design was made by

_____

Use complete sentences to explain your thinking.

_____

_____

V
PROBABILITY

27—The Color Spinner

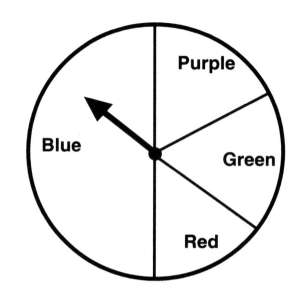

¹Rob, Patty, Betty and Gerry are playing a spinner game. ²Betty's favorite color is blue. ³Gerry's favorite color is green. ⁴Rob's favorite color is red. ⁵Patty's favorite color is purple. ⁶Any time the spinner lands on someone's favorite color, that person wins! ⁷When the game started Patty said, "This game is not fair." ⁸But since it was raining outside and they were bored, they played the game anyway.

Questions

1. How do you win at this game? Use complete sentences to explain your thinking.

   _____
   _____

2. What color is the pointer most likely to land on? _____ Use complete sentences to explain your thinking.

   _____
   _____

3. Who is most likely to win? _____

   Write the number of the sentence that gives the best evidence for your answer. _____

MATH DETECTIVE Beginning   Probability

4. What are Betty's odds, or chances, of winning each time they spin?

   a. 1/4
   b. 1/3
   c. 1/2
   d. 1

5. Does Rob's favorite color have the same first letter as that of his first name? _____

   Write the number of the sentence that gives the best evidence for your answer. _____

6. What are Rob's odds of winning each time they spin?

   a. 0
   b. 1/6
   c. 1/4
   d. 1/3

7. Why did the children play the game even though some of them thought it was unfair? Use complete sentences to explain your thinking.

   _____

   _____

   Write the number of the sentence that gives the best evidence for your answer. _____

8. 🎉 Why did Patty say this game was not fair? Use complete sentences to explain your thinking.

   _____

   _____

9. Is it possible that someone else won, other than the one most likely to win (from question 3)? Use complete sentences to explain your thinking.

   _____

   _____

28—The Ice Cream Party

¹Ms. Kamen wanted to have an ice cream party for her class of twenty students. ²She bought four half-gallons. ³She bought chocolate, strawberry, chocolate chip, and vanilla. ⁴She also bought two packages of sugar cones. ⁵She told each student that they could each have only 2 scoops. ⁶Each student had a cone with two different flavors. ⁷Each half-gallon cost $4.00. ⁸Each package of cones cost $1.50.

```
c = chocolate
s = strawberry
v = vanilla
p = chocolate chip
```

Questions

1. Using the key shown above, list all the possible cones a student could have made using two different flavors. (A cone with vanilla first and then chocolate is the same as a cone with chocolate first and then vanilla).

   How many different cones were possible to make? _____

2. What are the odds that the first student would pick a cone with strawberry and vanilla? _____ Use complete sentences to explain your thinking.
   _____
   _____

3. Did anyone have a cone with two scoops of vanilla? _____

   Write the number of the sentence that gives the best evidence for your answer. _____

4. If every student had ice cream and Ms. Kamen had none, how many scoops were served?

   a. 40 scoops
   b. 20 scoops
   c. 10 scoops
   d. 80 scoops

5. How many gallons of ice cream did Ms. Kamen buy? _____.

   Write the number of the sentence that gives the best evidence for your answer. _____

6. How much did Ms. Kamen spend on ice cream and cones? Show your work, labelling and organizing your information.

29—Summer Reading

¹At the public library, the librarian has chosen these books for children to read. ²Each child must read two books, one from each of the two categories, to win a special sticker.

Adventure	Biography
Wild Ponies (P)	Leon's Story (L)
The Girl Who Went to Mars (M)	Benjamin Franklin (F)
	Helen Thayer (T)

Questions

1. What does a child have to do to win a special sticker? From the above lists, he or she must read

   a. any four books.
   b. one Adventure book and one Biography book.
   c. any two Biography books.
   d. two Adventure books and two Biography books.

   Write the number of the sentence that gives the best evidence for your answer. _____

2. Melissa has already read Benjamin Franklin and does not want to read it again. List the different choices she can make to get a sticker. Use the abbreviations next to each book to make it easier to list them.

3. Luis does not want to read The Girl Who Went to Mars. List the different choices he has to get a sticker. Use the abbreviations to make it easier to list.

4. Lushima hasn't read any of the books on the list. How many possible choices does he have?_____ You may use connecting lines to help you show the possible combinations.

5. What are the odds that Lushima will pick Wild Ponies and Helen Thayer to get his first sticker?_____ Use complete sentences to explain your thinking.

_____
_____
_____

30—The Missing Symbols

¹Ms. Kamen wrote the symbols +, −, ×, and ÷ on cards and put the cards in a box. ²She shook the box and asked a student in her class to draw out a card. ³Ms. Kamen said that the student who drew the card with the division symbol and placed it in the right equation would win two candy bars. ⁴Any student who drew a card with another symbol and placed it in the right equation would win one candy bar. ⁵Amy said, "I hope I get the division symbol!" ⁶Ms. Kamen put the following equations on the board.

A. 12 ◯ 3 = 4

B. 12 ◯ 3 = 9

C. 3 ◯ 12 = 36

D. 4 ◯ 3 = 7

Questions

Fill in the circles above with the correct symbols as you answer the questions below.

1. Without looking at the cards, Marcos pulled one from the box. What were the odds (chances) that he would get card with the division symbol? _____

2. Marcos got the addition symbol and placed it in the right equation. The card stayed outside of the box. Write the letter of the equation he placed it on. _____

3. It was Luis's turn. What were his odds of getting the division symbol now? _____ Use complete sentences to explain your thinking.

_____

_____

4. Luis got the subtraction symbol and placed it in the right equation. The symbol stayed outside of the box. Write the letter of the equation he placed it in. _____.

5. Now, it was Mary's turn. What were her odds of getting the division symbol? _____ Use complete sentences to explain your thinking.

_____

_____

6. Mary got the division symbol but placed it in the wrong equation. She had to put the symbol back in the box and sit down. Now, what were Amy's odds of getting the division symbol?
   a. Less than Mary's because the division symbol came out once and it's not likely to come out again.
   b. Greater than Mary's because Amy was the person who really wanted to win the two candy bars.
   c. The same as Mary's, since there were two symbols in the box again.
   d. Zero, since there were no longer any division symbols in the box.

7. Amy got the division symbol and placed it in the right equation. The symbol stayed outside of the box. Write the letter of the equation she put it in. _____

8. It was Eddie's turn. What were the odds that he would get a candy bar? _____ Use complete sentences to explain your thinking.

_____

_____

9. Who won the most candy bars?
   a. Eddie
   b. Marcos
   c. Mary
   d. Amy

10. Play your own Missing Symbols game. Cut out the symbols at the bottom of the page and put them in a box. Play as described in the story.

The Missing Symbols Game

A. 12 ◯ 3 = 4

B. 12 ◯ 3 = 9

C. 3 ◯ 12 = 36

D. 4 ◯ 3 = 7

Cutouts:

VI
STATISTICS

31—Mrs. Applecrumb's Famous Fruit Pies

¹Mrs. Applecrumb spends the whole week baking pies. ²On Sundays, she sells them at the Farmers Market. ³People come from all over to buy her delicious, flaky pies.

⁴One day, her nephew Simon began to draw a pictograph of how many fruit pies Mrs. Applecrumb sold right before Thanksgiving. ⁵He asked his aunt how many cherry pies she sold. ⁶She said, "I sold eleven cherry pies." ⁷Simon never finished graphing the cherry pies because he was busy eating the ones she didn't sell!

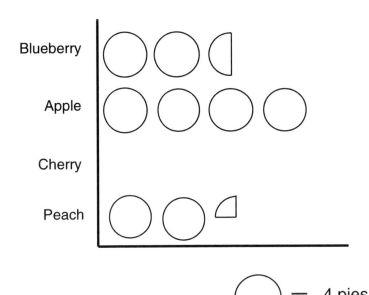

Questions

1. How many apple pies did she sell?

    a. 4
    b. 8
    c. 16
    d. 12

2. In the graph above, graph the number of cherry pies Mrs. Applecrumb sold.

    Write the number of the sentence that gives the best evidence for your answer. _____

3. How many peach pies did she sell?
   a. 9
   b. 2 and 3 slices
   c. 5
   d. 10

4. How many more apple pies did she sell than blueberry pies? _____ Show your work.

5. a. Fill out the chart to show how many pies Mrs. Applecrumb sold.

   b. If Mrs. Applecrumb sold each pie for $6.00, how much money did she make that day?_____ Show your work.

Blueberry	
Apple	
Cherry	
Peach	
Total Sold	

6. At $6.00 a pie, how many pies would Mrs. Applecrumb have to sell to make $300.00? _____ Show your work.

32—Tully Tallies Temper Tantrums

	Reason	Tally
A	"When my parents make me go to bed early"	||||
B	"When my older brother or sister is on the phone too long"	𝍶
C	"When someone breaks a promise"	𝍶 𝍶 |||
D	"When I'm blamed for something I did not do"	𝍶 𝍶

[1]Tully asked his friends what makes them most upset. [2]He asked them to vote for only one of the reasons on the list above. [3]He then kept a tally of what each friend answered. [4]Later, Tully made the bar graph below.

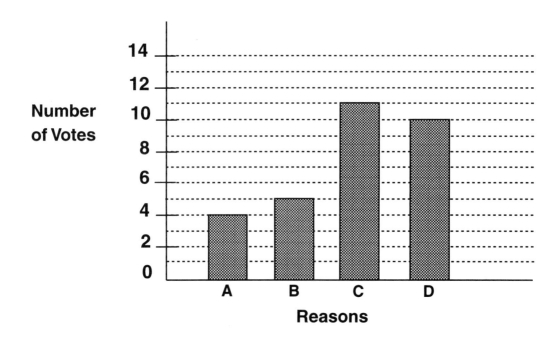

Questions

1. Look carefully at Tully's graph. What mistake did Tully make on his graph? Use complete sentences to explain your thinking.

   _____

   _____

2. What, if anything, did Tully forget to put on his graph?

   a. A name for the vertical axis (up & down).
   b. A name for the horizontal axis (across).
   c. A title for the graph.
   d. None of the above.

3. How many times did each friend vote for a reason on Tully's list? _____

   Write the number of the sentence that gives the best evidence for your answer. _____

4. 🎏 What would make the best title for the graph?

   a. What My Friends Enjoy
   b. Who Makes Me Maddest
   c. What Rules Parents Should Follow
   d. What Makes My Friends Upset

5. Why did Tully pick a bar graph and not a line graph?

   a. A bar graph is used to compare different kinds of data.
   b. A bar graph is the best way to compare data over a period of time.
   c. A bar graph is always easier to make than a line graph.
   d. Tully said he didn't know how to make a line graph.

33—The Pet Shelter

¹The line graph below shows the number of pets that were adopted from August through January. ²Mrs. Trumbull, the owner of the pet shelter, said on TV that more people adopt pets from November through January than from August through October. ³She also said that giving pets as gifts is a good idea only if the person getting the pet really wants a pet and can take good care of it.

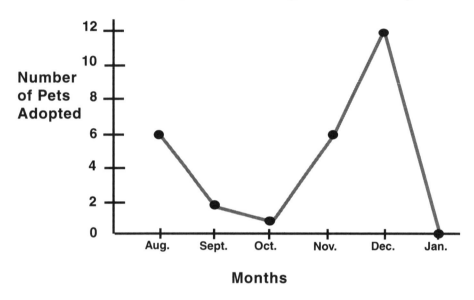

Pets Adopted from August to January

Questions

1. Based on the evidence shown on this graph, was Mrs. Trumbull right in saying that more people adopt pets from November through January? Use complete sentences to explain your thinking.

   _____

   _____

2. How many more pets were adopted in December compared to August? _____ Show your work.

3. Would Mrs. Trumbull think it's a good idea to give a pet to someone who is away from home most of the time? _____

   Write the number of the sentence that gives the best evidence for your answer. _____

4. How many pets were adopted from August to January? _____ Show your work.

5. Which two months show the same number of pets being adopted? _____, _____

6. We see the biggest increase (or rise) in pet adoptions
   a. from October to November.
   b. from November to December.
   c. from August to September.
   d. from December to January.

7. We see the biggest decrease (or drop) in pet adoptions
   a. from August to September
   b. from September to October.
   c. from October to November.
   d. from December to January.

8. Why do you think Mrs. Trumbull used a line graph instead of a bar graph for her report? Use complete sentences to explain your thinking.

   _____

   _____

34—The Great Fruit Sale

¹Students at Glenwood Elementary School are selling boxes of oranges to raise money for a new playground. ²They have 150 boxes to sell. ³Each box of fruit has 3 dozen oranges. ⁴Each box sells for $10.00. ⁵Every box that was sold on Monday was bought by a teacher in the school. ⁶Every teacher bought one box on Monday. ⁷On Wednesday, the school had an open house for parents at 7 P.M. ⁸Saturday, the students sold boxes at the mall.

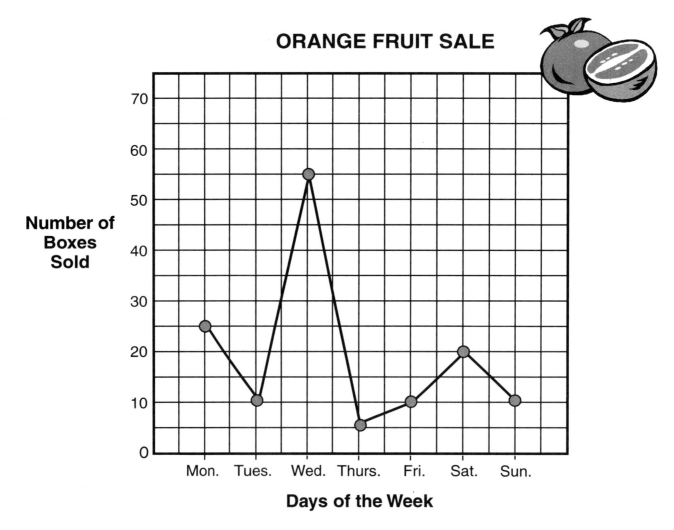

Questions

1. How many oranges are there in 3 dozen? _____

2. How many teachers are in the school? _____

   Write the numbers of the two sentences that give the best evidence for your answer. _____, _____

MATH DETECTIVE Beginning   Statistics

3. On which day did the students sell the most fruit? _____

4. Why were so many boxes of fruit sold on that day? Use complete sentences to explain your thinking.
   _____
   _____

5. On which days did the students sell the same amount of boxes?
   _____

6. What could be a reason why more boxes of fruit were sold on Saturday than on Friday or Sunday? Use complete sentences to explain your thinking.
   _____
   _____

7. What was the total number of boxes sold from Monday to Sunday? _____ Show your work.

8. How many boxes were not sold? _____ Show your work.

   Write the number of the sentence that gives the best evidence for your answer. _____

9. What was the third highest selling day? _____

10. How much money was made during all seven days? _____ Show your work.

   Write the number of the sentence that gives the best evidence for your answer. _____

© 2003 Critical Thinking Books & Software • www.CriticalThinking.com • 800-458-4849   77

35—Time for Homework

[1]Cody's mom made a graph of the number of minutes Cody spent doing his homework. [2]One day Cody spent a total of one-half hour doing his math homework. [3]Another day, Cody took over one hour to make a science poster, which was due the next day. [4]On Friday, Cody did not do any homework. [5]On the other two days of the week, Cody spent the same amount of time doing his homework.

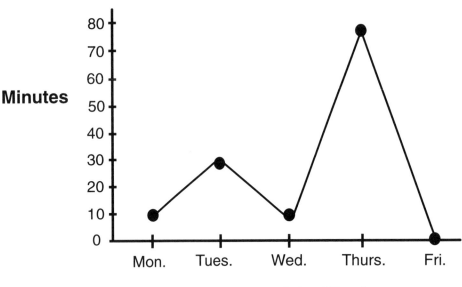

Questions

1. On which day of the week did Cody work on math homework?_____

    Write the number of the sentence that (along with the graph) gives the best evidence for your answer. _____

2. On which day of the week did Cody work on his poster?_____

    Write the number of the sentence that (along with the graph) gives the best evidence for your answer. _____

3. On which two days did Cody spend the same amount of time doing homework?

   a. Monday and Friday
   b. Monday and Thursday
   c. Monday and Wednesday
   d. Tuesday and Wednesday

4. How much more time did Cody spend making his poster than doing his math homework? _____ Show your work.

5. How much time altogether did Cody spend that week doing his homework? Change your answer to hours and minutes. _____ Show your work.

6. Cody's mom wants Cody to spend a total of 5 hours the following week doing homework. How much more time does Cody need to put into his homework to make his mom happy? _____ Show your work.

36—Zooey Competition

¹Zoo World is the new zoo in town. ²A person from Zoo World said on TV that they have more popular animals in their zoo than Zoo City. ³Zoo City is the old zoo on the other side of town. ⁴Zoo City also said they have many popular animals at their zoo. ⁵Both zoos printed the graphs below in the newspaper. ⁶When people saw both graphs in the newspaper, many believed that Zoo World had more popular animals.

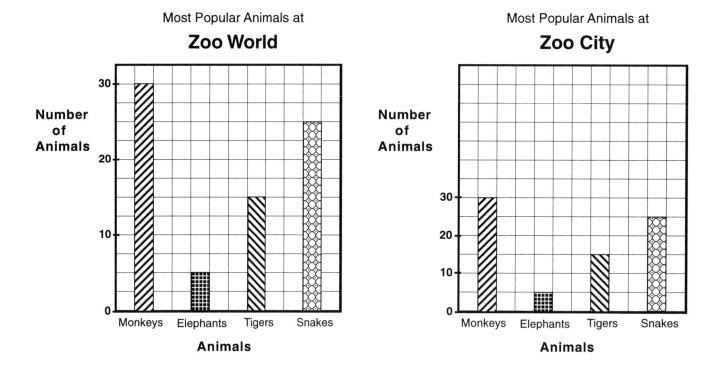

Questions

1. Which zoo is telling everyone that they have more popular animals?
   _____.

   Write the number of the sentence that gives the best evidence for your answer. _____

2. Carefully study the graphs and fill out the number of popular animals that are in each zoo.

Zoo World		Zoo City	
Monkeys	_____	Monkeys	_____
Elephants	_____	Elephants	_____
Tigers	_____	Tigers	_____
Snakes	_____	Snakes	_____
Total	_____	Total	_____

3. Do you think Zoo World is correct when they say that they have more popular animals than Zoo City? _____ Use complete sentences to explain your thinking.

_____

_____

4. Why do you think someone might make a mistake when comparing numbers of popular animals in the zoos? Use complete sentences to explain your thinking.

_____

_____

37—The Basset Hound Bus Company

[1]The Basset Hound Bus Company buses travel each morning from downtown to Cass Park Swimming Pool. [2]There are five buses that make this trip each day during the summer months. [3]Here is the schedule showing when each bus leaves downtown. [4]Bus 5 is the only bus that goes straight from Cass Park to the zoo.

The Basset Hound Bus Schedule
Safety is our concern

	Leaves	Arrives
Bus 1	7:20	7:45
Bus 2	8:20	8:45
Bus 3	9:20	9:45
Bus 4	10:20	10:45
Bus 5	11:20	11:45

Questions

1. All the buses in the Basset Hound Bus Company travel

    a. from downtown to the zoo.
    b. from downtown to Cass Park Swimming Pool.
    c. from Cass Park Swimming Pool to the zoo.
    d. from the zoo to the pool.

    Write the number of the sentence that gives the best evidence for your answer. _____

2. According to the schedule above, how long does it take to get from downtown to Cass Park?
    a. 15 minutes
    b. 20 minutes
    c. 2 hours
    d. 25 minutes

MATH DETECTIVE Beginning   Statistics

3. How often does the bus leave downtown?

   a. every hour
   b. every half-hour
   c. every 25 minutes
   d. every 10 minutes

4. If Tom doesn't want to be late for his swimming lesson at 9:40 A.M., what is the last bus he can take from downtown?

   a. Bus 2
   b. Bus 3
   c. Bus 4
   d. Bus 5

   Use complete sentences to explain your thinking.

   _____

   _____

5. Tom's lesson starts at 9:40 A.M. and lasts half an hour. What time is his lesson over? _____ Show your work.

6. In six minutes, Bus 4 is due to arrive at Cass Park. The bus is never late. What time is it now?

   a. 10:46
   b. 10:39
   c. 9:31
   d. 10:06

7. It takes Bus 5 five minutes to unload the passengers at Cass Park and twenty-five minutes to get from Cass Park to the zoo. What time does it get to the zoo? _____ Show your work.

38—The Shoe Count

¹Maggie, Sarah, and Nik each have six pairs of shoes. ²Maggie and Sarah have the same number of pairs of sneakers. ³Maggie has two pairs of sandals. ⁴Sarah has twice as many pairs of sneakers as pairs of black shoes, but she has no sandals. ⁵Nik has half as many pairs of sandals as Maggie. ⁶Sarah and Nik have the same number of pairs of black shoes.

Pairs of

	Sneakers	Black Shoes	Sandals
Maggie			
Sarah			
Nik			

Questions

1. What is the total number of pairs of shoes owned by all three children? _____

    Write the number of the sentence that gives the best evidence for your answer. _____

2. Fill out the chart above to help you answer the following questions. Go back and read and reread all the clues again to make sure your chart is correct. (Remember: to be a good math detective, you must be a careful reader!)

3. How many pairs of sandals does Maggie have? _____

   Write the number of the sentence that gives the best evidence for your answer. _____

4. 🚩 Sarah has twice as many pairs of sneakers as pairs of black shoes and she has no pairs of sandals. How could you find out how many pairs of sneakers and pairs of black shoes Sarah has? Use complete sentences to explain your thinking.

   _____

   _____

5. 🚩 How did you get the answer to how many pairs of sneakers Nik has? Use complete sentences to explain your thinking.

   _____

   _____

6. 🚩 Graph your results from the chart on page 84. Show a comparison of the totals for all three types of shoes. Add a title, and label both axes. (Make it clear whether you are graphing *pairs* of shoes or *numbers* of shoes.)

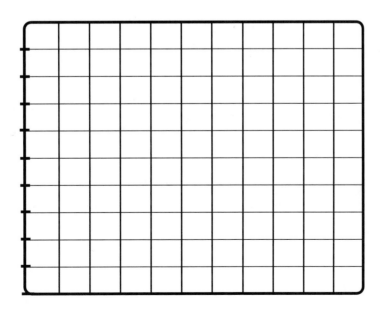

ANSWERS

NOTE: Given in parentheses are extra explanations not required of the student. Answers (outside parentheses except where needed to show coordinates or order of operations) show correct student responses to the questions, though wordings may vary. Accept responses with the same meaning. You may use the Rubric described on page x for scoring answers.

I. NUMBER & NUMERATION

1—Latoya's Vacation, p. 1

1. August 19th. Sentences 1 and 2.
2. 15 days.
3. a. Sentence 3.
4. 2 Broadway, 3 Cousins, 1 Statue of Liberty.
5. August 24th. Sentence 6.
6. b.
7. b.
8. d. We don't know if she travelled by car, bus, train, plane, ship, or other.

2—Eddy's Dog Shadow, p. 4

1. a, b:

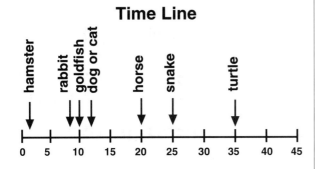

2. d.
3. b. Sentences 2 and 3.
4. c.
5. a.
6. a.

7. He did not want to be sad if another pet died. Answers may vary.
8. No. A turtle lives a lot longer than a horse, and it's a lot smaller. Some small animals, like hamsters, have a shorter life-span than bigger animals, like dogs. Examples given may vary.

3—Who's Telling The Truth?, p. 6

1. c. Sentences 3 and 4. (x means multiply.)
2. a. Sentences 6 and 7. (+ means add.)
3. b. Sentence 7. (- means subtract.)
4. d. Sentence 5. (÷ means divide by.)
5. Jing: 8 x 30 is 240, so 8 x 31 has to be more than 240.
   Lani: 16 ÷ 4 = 4, so 17 ÷ 4 has to be more than 4.
6. a.
7. Adding 49 to 495 will give you a bigger number than taking 49 away from 495.
8. d.

4—School Supplies, p. 8

CHART—Tom: $21.00. Luis: $8.00. Mary: $30.00. Tina: $48.00. (Eight packages of markers times $6.00 each is $48.) John: $17.00.

1. a. Sentence 3. (The number 17 is the only prime number on the list. A prime number has only two factors, one and itself.)
2. b. Sentence 4. (8 is the only factor of 24 on the chart.)
3. c. Sentence 6. (The number 10 is a factor of 30.)
4. $9. ($30 - $21 = $9)
5. $124. ($21 + $8 + $30 + $48 + $17 = $124)
6. 1, 2, 3, 5, 6, 15 and 30. (Factors of 30 other than 10.)

5—At the Math Fair, p. 10

1. *Sum* means the answer to addition.
2. c. (17 + 18 = 25)
3. b. Sentence 10. (Choice d is wrong because both 20 and 18 are even numbers.)
4. a. Sentence 4. (Remember, Sammy thinks two odd numbers add up to an odd number.)
5. No. [17 + 17 = 34. The number 34 is not odd.] (Accept any correct equation adding two odd numbers.)
6. No. [18 + 20 = 38. The number 38 is not odd.] (Accept any correct equation adding two even numbers.)
7. c.
8. a. even.
   b. even.
   c. odd.

6—The Super Deli, p. 12

1. c.
2. $4.00. Sentences 4 and 7.
3. d.
4. a. (Sentence 8 says one of them spent $7.00. The other two spent about $3.00 and $4.00.)
5. b. (Remember, she doesn't like turkey—sentence 3. She must have been the one who spent $7.00, so it can't be d.)
6. About $34. (6 x $4.00 = $24.00; 5 x $2.00 = $10.00; $24.00 + $10.00 = $34.00)

7—The Party Favors, p. 14

1. 4. Sentence 1.
2. a. Sentence 3.
3. a.

4. | Favors | Favors/3 (# per friend) | Remainder |
   |--------|-------------------------|-----------|
   | 25 | 8 | 1 |
   | 24 | 8 | 0 |
   | 23 | 7 | 2 |
   | 22 | 7 | 1 |
   | 21 | 7 | 0 |
   | 20 | 6 | 2 |
   | 19 | 6 | 1 |

5. 2, 0. (See the pattern of 0, 1, 2 in Remainder column.)
6. a. 18 ÷ 3 = 6 R 0 or 24 ÷ 3 = 3 R 0
7. 2, 1, or 0

8—The Five Wealthy Women, p. 16

1. b. Sentence 4.
2. Wednesday. Sentences 4 and 5.
3. d. Sentence 5.
4. Thursday. (One day after Antonia, which was two days after Monday, sentences 4–6.)
5. $70,700.
6. $70,070.
7. Friday. (See sentences 4–8.)
8. c.
9. $35,003,850. Sentences 8 and 9. ($7,000,770 x 5)
10. | Thurs. | Ali | $70,070 |
    | Thurs. | Andrea | $70,700 |
    | Wed. | Antonia | $700,000 |
    | Mon. | Anna | $7,000,000 |
    | Fri. | Abby | $7,000,770 |
    | | Total | $14,841,540 |

9—Leafy Lengths, p. 18

1.

2. D, C, A. Sentence 4.

3. F, E, B. Sentence 3.

II. PATTERNS

10—The Family Tree, p. 20

1. (Note: spouses can be given in reversed order as long as each person remains with the correct parent and/or child.)

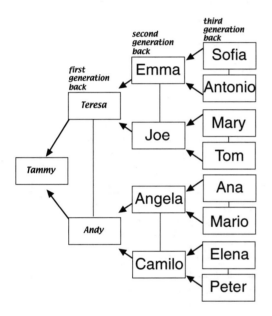

2. Yes, her grandmother Emma helped her. Sentences 3 and 4.

3. 3.

4. Emma's mother and father OR Sofia and Antonio. Sentences 9 and 10.

5. Great Grampa Mario. Sentence 13.

6. Mary and Tom. (See sentences 7 and 8.)

7. Andy.

8. 8, 16, 32. Each number is doubled from the one before.

9. 63. 1 + 2 + 4 + 8 + 16 + 32 = 63

11—Trip to the Theater, p. 22

1. Chart should be symmetrical, as below.

2. 18 seats. (17 students plus herself) Sentence 5.

3. 14. Sentence 3.

4. No. Sentence 6.

5. Row 7. In row 7 there are 18 seats, which is exactly the number they need. (One seat for Ms. Kamen and 17 for her students—see question 2.)

6. Sentence 7. $39. $17 X 2 = $34; $34 + $5 = $39. ($5.00 for Ms. Kamen and 17 children at $2.00 each.)

7. 150 seats. 6 + 8 + 10 + 12 + 14 + 16 + 18 + 20 + 22 + 24 = 150. (The theater has 10 rows.)

8. $420. 40 adults x $5.00 = $200; 150 – 40 = 110 children; 110 children x $2.00 = $220; $200 + $220 = $420.

12—The Toy Factory, p. 24

1.

Number of Figures	Teddy Bear Buttons	Action Hero Buttons	Total Buttons
1	3	5	8
2	6	10	16
3	9	15	24
4	12	20	32
5	15	25	40
6	18	30	48
7	21	35	56
8	24	40	64
9	27	45	72
10	30	50	80

2. 8. (3 + 5 = 8) Sentences 2 and 3.
3. 30 minutes. Sentence 1.
4. 64 buttons. 100 – 36 = 64. Sentence 7.
5. a. (Subtract 36 from the 100 buttons we started with to find that 64 buttons were used. From the chart, we see that 8 of each figure would require 24 + 40 = 64 buttons.)
6. Five teddy bears and 5 action heroes. Five teddy bears need a total of 15 buttons, and 5 action heroes need 25 buttons. 15 + 25 = 40 buttons.

13—The 35¢ Yummy Bar, p. 26

1. Maria. 7 coins. Sentence 5.
2. 4 coins. Sentence 6 and 8.
3. 2 coins.
4. The machine takes nickels, dimes, and quarters because it takes only exact change for 35¢ and does not take pennies. Sentences 1 and 2.
5.
Name	#	Types of coins
Maria	7	5 + 5 + 5 + 5 + 5 + 5 + 5
Louisa	6	10 + 5 + 5 + 5 + 5 + 5
Melissa	5	10 + 10 + 5 + 5 + 5
Kevin	4	10 + 10 + 10 + 5
Sue	3	25 + 5 + 5
Dave	2	25 + 10

III. OPERATIONS

14—The City Bus, p. 30

1. c. Sentence 8.
2. No. Sentence 2.
3. 10. (50 – 40 = 10) Sentences 1 and 3.
4. 25. (40 – 15 = 25) Sentences 3 and 4.
5. 25. 50 – 25 = 25 (Number of seats minus number of people.)
6. 18. 25 + 10 – 3 = 32; 50 – 32 = 18 (Add people after 2nd stop and people picked up at 3rd; subtract people getting off at 3rd stop; subtract from number of seats.)
7. a. No. There are only 18 seats left empty after the third stop.

b.

Stop #	Get on	Get off	# On bus	Empty seats
One	40	0	40	10
Two	0	15	25	25
Three	10	3	32	18
Four	18	0	50	0

15—Eddy's Achy Ride. p. 32

1. 12. Sentence 5. (6 + 6 = 12)
2. 24. (12 x 2 = 24)
3. 4. 12 ÷ 3 = 4
4.

	How many sold?		How many eaten?	
At Kiki's	5		On the way to Kiki's	0
At Frankie's	10		On the way to Frankie's	6
At Emma's	20		On the way to Emma's	12
At the park	40		At the park	4
TOTAL	75		TOTAL	22

5. 100. 75 sold + 22 eaten + 3 left = 100 cookies.
6. $1.00. $75.00 ÷ 75 = $1.00. (He sold 75 cookies and had $75.00.)
7. a. (Sentence 17 supports this.)

16—An Apple a Day, p. 34

Name	Servings	Number of Chips	Grams of Fat	Calories
Zoe	(1)	(15)	10	150
Tyler	(2)	30	20	300
Eddy	4	60	40	600

1. b.
2. b.

3. d.
4. d.
5. 300. 600 – 300 = 300.
6. 84. 150 – 66 = 84.
7. (Answers may vary.) Potato chips have a lot of fat and also a lot of calories. Too much fat and too many calories are not healthy.

17—Time to Buy a New Clock, p. 36

1. $21.99. Sentence 5.
2. $20.29. $17.50 + $2.79 = $20.29. Sentences 7 and 8.
3. The green clock. The green clock is $21.99 and the blue clock with the battery is $20.29.
4. c. Sentence 9.
5. Wrapping paper. Sentence 10.
6. Yes. No. Dave has $25, so he has enough money for the blue clock, one battery, and the wrapping paper, which cost $24.29 altogether. The green clock and the wrapping paper cost $25.99.
7. No. Sentence 11.
8. The green clock. It costs $21.99. The blue clock with two batteries is $23.08.

18—The Toy Sale, p. 38

1. b. (Choice a would be $20 too, but John can't buy the tractor.) Sentence 3.
2. Luis must have bought the video game for $17.00, since he got $3 back from his $20.
3. a. (Choice b is wrong because the puzzles and games were already bought by John; choice a is the only other option that adds up to $20.)
4. $27.00. $50 – $23 = $27
5. <u>New price of bike</u>   <u>Change</u>
    $46.00 $54
   $54 – $8 = $46; $100 – $46 = $54
6. (One possible grouping follows.)
   $6.00 + $14 = $20; $23 + $17 = $40; $13 + $7 = $20. $20 + $40 + $20 = $80.00. (You can add quickly if you add by grouping pairs that result in multiples of 10.)

19—Dinner with Ramón, p. 40

1. $7.50. $9.50 – $2.00 = $7.50 (The chicken dinner was $9.50, but it's on special for $2.00 off the regular price.) Sentence 2.
2. $10.70. $7.50 + $3.20 = $10.70 (Add the costs of the chicken dinner and the apple pie.) Sentence 3.
3. $16.00. $13.50 + $2.50 = $16.00. (Add the costs of the steak and the flan.) Sentence 4.
4. 70 cents. $3.20 – $2.50 = .70 (The apple pie minus the flan.)
5. (The error is that the flan is $2.50 and not $4.50.)

Arroz con Pollo	$ **7.50**
Bistec	$ **13.50**
Apple Pie	$ 3.20
Flan	$ **2.50**
Total	$ **26.70**

20—Mr. Papas at the Toy Store, p. 42

1.
	A.M.	P.M.
Mon.	5 1/2	3 1/2
Tues.	4 1/2	4 1/2
Wed.	5	4 1/2
Thurs.	5 1/2	3 1/2
Fri.	3 1/2	2 1/2
Total A.M., P.M.	24	18 1/2

   Total hours (week): 42 1/2
2. 9 hours. 5 1/2 + 3 1/2 = 9 (6:30 to noon is 5 1/2 hours; 12:30 to 4:00 is 3 1/2 hours)
3. Wednesday. 9 1/2 hours. (5 + 4 1/2 = 9)
4. No. Some days he takes a half-hour for his lunch break, and other times he takes one hour.

5. 42 1/2. 24 (A.M.) + 18 (P.M.) = 42 1/2
6. $425.00. 42 1/2 × $10 = $425. Sentence 3. (85/2 × 10/1 = 425)
7. 36 hours. $360 ÷ $10 = 36
8. 2 1/2 hours. (42 1/2 − 40 = 2 1/2)
9. $450.00. 40 × $10 = $400
   2 1/2 × $20 = $50
   $400 + $50 = $450.00

IV. GEOMETRY

21—Off to the State Fair, p. 46

1. a. B (1,1)
      C (1,6)
      D (3,3)
      E (8,7)
      F (4,9)
      G (6,9)
   b. Points should be labelled as below:

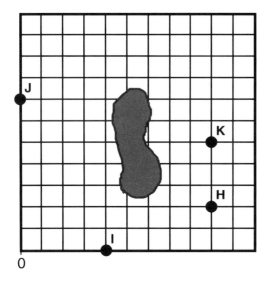

2. Starting at the point (0,0), you go over 9 units to the right and then 2 units up. Sentence 10.
3. 5.
4. 2.
5. 9 units.
6. At the Information Booth (B). Sentence 4.

22—Luis's Letter, p. 48

1. (See grid below.) Sentences 1 and 2.

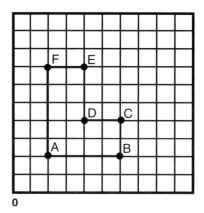

2. 4 units.
3. 18 units. I added all the units around the outside of the letter.
4. 14 square units. I counted all the units inside the letter OR I broke the figure into two parts and found length times width and added both parts. Sentence 6.
5. No. You get the perimeter by adding the unit lengths around the letter, and you get the area by adding up the square units inside the letter.

23—Annie's Angles Report, p. 50

1. b. Sentence 8.
2. c. Sentence 14.
3. acute. Sentence 9.
4. 90 degrees.
5. A straight line has 180 degrees because it is made up of two right angles. (90° + 90° = 180°)
6. (See sentence 16.)

7. Luis. Four 90-degree angles make a full circle. (90° x 4 = 360°, which is the same as turning 90° four times; you can also get a circle with 45° x 8, 180° x 2, etc.)

24—Trip to the Skating Rink, p. 52

1. Market Avenue. Sentences 1 and 2.
2. Lucy.
3. Tony. Sentence 4.
4. Thomas Avenue.
5. c.
6. d.
7. Grape and Thomas Avenues.
8. Park and Tenth Streets.
9. From Market Avenue to the swimming pool you have to take one-way streets, so Mrs. Ross has no choice but to go around the park.

25—The Pastry Shop, p. 54

1. b. Sentence 6 and 14.
2. b. Sentence 5 and 11.
3. Melissa. Sentences 4 and 16.
4. a. Sentence 12.
5. d. Sentences 7 and 15.

Word	cylinder	cube	sphere	cone	pyramid
Dessert	brown bread	cake	candy	ice cream cone	chocolate fudge
Who	Ada	Melissa	Eddy	Lucy	Tammy

26—Geometry Art, p.57

1. To complete the chart:
   nonagon <u>9 sides</u>
   decagon <u>10 sides</u>
2. c. (Emily is using 6-sided polygons so she must be using hexagons.)
3. d. (Amanda is using 3-sided polygons or triangles and she is using 8-sided polygons or octagons; she is NOT using pentagons.)
4. (Left:) Amanda. (Right:) Emily. Amanda is using octagons, or 8-sided polygons and triangles, or 3-sided polygons. Emily is using 6-sided polygons, or hexagons.

V. PROBABILITY

27—The Color Spinner, p. 60

1. In this game, you win by landing on your favorite color.
2. Blue. Blue takes up more space on the game board than any other color.
3. Betty. Sentence 2.
4. c. (Since her color covers 1/2 the game board, she has 1 out of 2 chances.)
5. Yes. Sentence 4.
6. b. (Since his color covers 1/6 of the game board, he has 1 out of 6 chances.)
7. They decided to play the game because it was raining outside, and they were bored. Sentence 8.
8. Patty said that this game was not fair because Betty's chances of winning were better than everyone else's. Blue took more space (one-half) on the spinner board than the others did!
9. Yes. The spinner could still land on other colors besides blue even though the odds of landing on blue are better.

28—The Ice Cream Party, p. 62

1. cs, cv, cp, sv, sp and vp. Six cones.
2. 1/6. There are six possible cones, so strawberry/vanilla is one of the six choices.
3. No. Sentence 6.
4. a. (20 X 2)
5. 2. (4 x 1/2) Sentence 2.
6. $19.00.
   ice cream: 4 X $4.00 = $16.00
   cones: 2 X $1.50 = $3.00
   altogether: $16.00 + $3.00 = $19.00

29—Summer Reading, p. 64

1. b. Sentence 2.
2. P and L; P and T; M and L; and M and T
3. P and L; P and F; and P and T
4. 6
5. 1/6. There are only six ways to choose one book from each of the two categories, so the odds of choosing any one of those ways are 1 out of 6.

30—The Missing Symbols, p. 66

Equations: A: ÷ B: − C: × D: +

1. one out of 4 OR 1/4.
2. D.
3. 1/3. There are only 3 symbols left. He has one chance out of the three.
4. 2.
5. 1/2. There are only two symbols left in the box, so her odds are 1 out of 2.
6. c. (one chance out of 2)
7. A.
8. 1 OR one out of one OR 100% (if the student knows the meaning of percents). There was only one symbol left and one equation left, so he would get the × symbol and place it in equation 3.
9. d.
10. (Missing Symbol game—outcomes will vary)

VI. STATISTICS

31—Mrs. Applecrumb's Famous Fruit Pies, p. 70

1. c. (4 × 4 = 16)
2. (Student should show 2 3/4 circles on the graph to represent 11 cherry pies.) Sentence 6.
3. a. (2 1/4 × 4 = 9)
4. 6. 16 apple − 10 blueberry = 6
5. a.

Blueberry	10
Apple	16
Cherry	11
Peach	9
TOTAL	46

   b. $276. 46 × $6 = $276
6. 50 pies. $300 ÷ $6.00 = 50

32—Tully Tallies Temper Tantrums, p. 72

1. Reason C is graphed incorrectly. The tally shows 13 for Reason 3, which should be graphed between 12 and 14.
2. c.
3. Once. Sentence 2.
4. d.
5. a.

33—The Pet Shelter, p. 74

1. Yes, 18 pets were adopted in November and December, and only 9 were adopted in August through October.
2. 6. 12 − 6 = 6
3. No. Sentence 3.
4. 27. 6 + 2 + 1 + 6 + 12 + 0 = 27
5. August, November. (Six pets were adopted in each month.)
6. b.
7. d.
8. Line graphs are used to show change over time.

34—The Great Fruit Sale, p. 76

1. 36. (3 × 12 = 36)
2. 25 teachers. Sentences 5 and 6.
3. Wednesday.
4. The school had an open house for parents (sentence 7). Parents probably bought a lot of fruit boxes.
5. Tuesday, Friday, and Sunday.

6. They sold boxes of fruits at the mall. There were probably more people at the mall.
7. 135. 25 + 10 + 55 + 5 + 10 + 20 + 10 = 135
8. 15. (150 - 135) Sentence 2.
9. Saturday.
10. $1350. 135 X $10. Sentence 4.

35—Time for Homework, p. 78

1. Tuesday. Sentence 2.
2. Thursday. Sentence 3.
3. c.
4. 50 minutes. 80 – 30 = 50.
5. 2 hours and 10 minutes.
   10 + 30 + 10 + 80 + 0 = 130 minutes
   130/60 = 2 10/60 = 2 hours 10 min.
6. 2 hours and 50 minutes.
   5 hours – 2 hours 10 minutes =
   4 hours 60 min. – 2 hours 10 min. =
   2 hours and 50 minutes.

36—Zooey Competition, p. 80

1. Zoo World. Sentence 2.
2.
	Zoo World	Zoo City
Monkeys	30	30
Elephants	5	5
Tigers	15	15
Snakes	25	25
TOTAL	75	75
3. No. Both zoos have the same number of each type of animal.
4. (Accept answers that show the following ideas.) The bars look taller because the scale was stretched out to make Zoo World look as if they had more popular animals. OR Fewer squares are used to show the same number OR In the Zoo World graph, it takes 4 squares to show 10, and in the Zoo City graph, it takes only 2 squares to show 10.

37—The Basset Hound Bus Company, p. 82

1. b. Sentence 1.
2. d. (45 – 20 = 25)
3. a.
4. a. Bus 2 arrives at 8:45. If he takes Bus 3 he would get there at 9:45 and be late.
5. 10:10 A.M. (9:40 + 30 = 10:10)
6. b. (10:45 – 6 = 10:39)
7. 12:15 P.M. (11:45 A.M. plus 5 minutes to unload is 11:50 A.M. Adding 25 more minutes to 11:50 A.M. gives 12:15 P.M.

38—The Shoe Count, p. 84

1. 18 pairs. (3 x 6 = 18) Sentence 1.
2.

Pairs of

	Sneakers	Black Shoes	Sandals
Maggie	4	0	2
Sarah	4	2	0
Nik	3	2	1

3. 2. Sentence 3.
4. Each person has 6 pairs of shoes. Sarah has no sandals. She has twice as many pairs of sneakers as black shoes. The only way to do this is to have 2 pairs of black shoes and 4 pairs of sneakers.
5. Nik has half as many sandals as Maggie (sentence 5), so he has one pair of sandals. Then because Nik and Sarah have the same number of black shoes (sentence 6), we know that Nik

has two pairs of black shoes. That leaves Nik with three pairs of sneakers, since each person has a total of 6 pairs of shoes.

6. (Graph should accurately reflect data shown in the answer to question 2. At the right is only one example. Another example could show groupings by shoe type instead of person.)

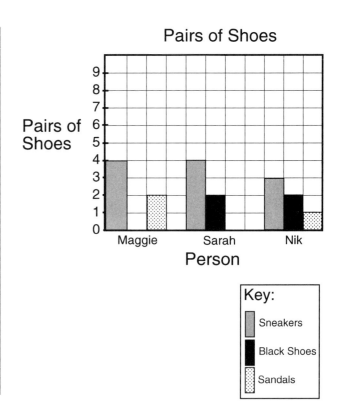

Teacher Notes

Teacher Notes